W9-BDL-004

101

THINGS YOU SHOULD KNOW HOW TO DO

101

THINGS YOU SHOULD KNOW HOW TO DO

Michael Powell

METRO BOOKS

NEW YORK

Publisher's Note

This book is for entertainment purposes only. Some of the activities discussed should not be attempted without professional supervision, or unless the reader has been properly trained or instructed in their technique.

Published exclusively for Metro Books by Gusto Company AS

© 2005 Gusto Company AS
Written by Michael Powell
Executive editor and original concept by James Tavendale
Designed by Allen Boe
Illustrated by Allen and AnnDréa Boe

ISBN-13: 978-1-4351-1026-7
1 3 5 7 9 10 8 6 4 2

Introduction

There's a right way and a wrong way to do everything, and then there's a better way. Just because you've been brushing your teeth for years, doesn't mean that you're doing it right. The same goes for pitching a baseball, packing a suitcase, or choosing a pair of sunglasses. Most of us are clueless when it comes to the simplest tasks. Did you know that some of the most basic life skills are the most poorly learned?

Then what about all those things you've always wished you could do but never got around to, like juggling, belly dancing, dancing the waltz, and making a shelter in the wild. And that's before you even consider the correct way to eat a lobster and choose a good pair of shoes.

Nothing is more important than getting back to basics! Nothing! That's why you'll love this book. It's an absolutely essential collection of clear and straightforward advice—everything you need to start coping with the miscellany of modern life. It even shows you how to get out of a chair, because—what do you know—we all screw that one up! The only thing we haven't included is how to suck eggs (although we do show you how to cook them and check if they are fresh).

This pocket-sized primer will help you maneuver the daily challenges of social etiquette, business, household management, home and family, relationships, health and hygiene, and sports and leisure. It will make you wonder how you ever dared get out of bed in the morning.

Contents

How To …

Speed-reading is an invaluable way of soaking up important information quickly and efficiently. When you need to read a mountain of material fast, there are several techniques at hand to help you cut down your reading time. Speed-reading is a skill that is much in demand in today's information-flooded age.

Know What You Want

The most important requirement is to decide what information you need to get from the document before you start to read it. If you need an overview, or the basic facts, you can read faster than if you need to understand and retain minute details.

Read Blocks Of Words

Most of us learn to read letter-by-letter, then word-by-word, but fewer of us take the next step and train ourselves to read blocks of words at a time. To speed-read you need to increase the number of words you can read in each block.

Avoid Regressing

Reading never progresses smoothly from left to right. Our eyes constantly flick back to a word or block of words to check meaning. While this is normal, excessive regressing is inefficient and has been shown to reduce comprehension as well as speed. It is also much more tiring for the eyes. Consciously reduce how much your eye regresses. This can be achieved initially by smoothly running a piece of paper line-by-line down the page, above the line of print as you read. Or, you can run your finger down the page faster than you would normally read and try to keep up with it.

Increase Your Eye Span

Simply holding the text slightly further away from you can dramatically increase your eye span.

Read Key Words

If you keep fixating on words like "the" or "and," then you need to concentrate on the key words of the sentence instead. Your brain should be able to recognize the filler words without fixating on them, leaving more time for focusing on the key words.

Read Silently

You may not be aware that you are doing it, but many people actually sound the words out in their throat or say them mentally. This is called "sub-vocalization" and it slows down reading considerably. Instead you should think the words, rather than speak or hear them. If you must sub-vocalize, do it just with the key words.

Learning to ride a bike can take minutes or a few hours, but it requires a little bit of courage and a trusted friend (to hold the bike steady and stop you from falling).

[1] Learn to ride when you are as young as possible. The older you get, the heavier you get, making it harder for your helper to hold the bike steady, chase after you, and catch you if you fall.

[2] Lower the seat so that you can touch the ground with your feet. You should be able to straddle the bike with both feet flat on the ground (not just tiptoes). When you are more confident with your balance, you can raise the seat.

[3] The first thing to master is balance. Practice on a large paved area, free from obstacles, so that you can concentrate on balance, without having to worry about steering or braking.

[4] At first your helper can steady the bike by holding onto the back of the seat and one side of the handlebars. Once you feel safe, your helper can gradually give less and less support, until finally letting go completely.

[5] As you build up speed and feel that you are balancing with very little help, have your friend release the bike, and run alongside you so that as soon as you start to slow down or falter, he or she can catch you if necessary. Stopping and starting is the most difficult part at this stage, so that's when you are likely to need most help.

[6] Keep pedaling. If you get wobbly, pedaling will help to restore balance.

[7] After you have mastered balance, focus on steering and braking. Remember to put your feet down after you brake so that the bike doesn't fall over. Use the back brake (rather than both together, otherwise the bike will stop too fast and you may be thrown forward over the handlebars).

[8] Always wear a helmet and learn the rules of the road, including never riding out into a road without stopping to check for traffic, obeying stop signs, and checking for traffic behind you, before turning or changing lanes.

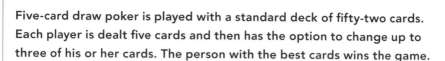
Five-card draw poker is played with a standard deck of fifty-two cards. Each player is dealt five cards and then has the option to change up to three of his or her cards. The person with the best cards wins the game.

It is possible to win with a weak hand (if you bluff everyone else into thinking you have a winning hand—more about that later), but there are nine winning patterns to aim for, in order from best to worst:

Royal Flush:
Ace, King, Queen, Jack, 10, all of the same suit.

Straight Flush:
Five cards of the same suit in numerical order. In a tie, the highest value card wins. If they are identical, the pot is shared. The Ace can count high or low, but not both, so for example K, A, 2, 3, 4 isn't allowed, but A, 2, 3, 4, 5 or 10, J, Q, K, A are valid.

Four of a Kind:
Four cards of the same value. In a tie, the cards with the highest value win.

Full House:
Three of one value, two of another. If two players have a full house, the higher value of the threesome wins.

Flush:
Five cards of the same suit. In a tie, the person with the highest value cards wins.

Straight:

Five cards of different suits in numerical order. Again, the Ace can count high or low, but not both, so, for example, Q, K, A, 2, 3 isn't allowed, whereas A, 2, 3, 4, 5 or 10, J, Q, K, A are valid.

Three of a Kind:

Three cards of the same value. If two players have three of a kind, the cards with the highest value win.

Two Pairs:

Two pairs of cards. In a tie the top value wins. If the top value is the same, the bottom value is next, followed by the value of the fifth card.

One Pair:

In a tie the highest value wins, followed by the next highest cards held.

Betting

Everyone puts an ante into the pot before the cards are dealt (this amount is agreed upon by players beforehand).

The dealer deals everyone five cards face down. Players look at their cards and betting begins with the first person to the left of the dealer. They can "bet" (placing any amount into the pot, up to the betting limit), "fold" (quit the game), or "check" (stay in the game, but wait for the next round to bet). Once a bet has been made, subsequent players must either "see" (match) the bet, "raise" (see first, then increase the bet), or "fold."

After the first round of betting, anyone who hasn't folded can exchange up to three cards from the dealer.

Betting resumes until there are no more raises, then everyone shows their cards, and the person with the best hand wins the pot.

Bluffing

Keeping a poker face and disguising your emotions is a big part of this game, but the most important skill is understanding what your opponents are thinking—trying to recognize the mannerisms that give them away and tell you the strength of their hand. Also, mix up your betting. If you bet conservatively, folding every poor hand, when you do eventually bet everyone will know you have a good hand. Try to think long-term, rather than about winning every time—the trick, when you have a good hand, is to encourage others to stay in the game.

Chess is a game played with two opposing armies of sixteen pieces each, on a board of alternating black and white squares. One army is black, the other is white. Players take turns to move one piece at a time, and the object of the game is to trap the opponent's king so that it is unable to move without being threatened.

No two pieces may occupy the same square at the same time. If a piece lands on an occupied square, the opposing piece is "taken" from the board.

Each player begins the game with a king, a queen, two rooks, two knights, two bishops, and eight pawns.

Set up the board like this, with a black square on the bottom left corner.

Moving the pieces

Each piece moves in a different way.

The knight moves in an L-shape, two squares in one direction and one square perpendicular to that. It is the only piece that can jump over pieces to reach its destination.

The bishop moves any number of squares, but diagonally only. One bishop moves on black squares, the other moves on white squares.

The rook moves any number of squares horizontally or vertically up and down the board.

The king moves one square at a time in any direction. He may "take" the opponent's pieces, but he must not land in a square that is threatened by his opponent.

The queen can move any number of squares in any direction (but cannot jump over other pieces).

A pawn moving for the first time can go one or two squares forward. After that it can only move one square forward, except when it is taking an opposing piece, which moves it forward one square diagonally. If a pawn reaches the other end of the board it is promoted into any piece the player chooses (usually a queen).

Check

When a player moves a piece into a position that threatens the opposing king, the king is in check. The other player must immediately eliminate this threat, either by blocking the opposing piece, taking it, or moving the king out of check. If this is not possible, the king is in "checkmate" and the player loses the game.

Castling

If a king and rook have not moved yet and there are empty squares between them, the player may perform a "castling" move, but only once during the game. This involves moving the king first so that it is next to the rook, then moving the rook to the other side of the king. You cannot castle to get out of check, nor can the king pass through check during the maneuver.

It's a draw

Sometimes the game ends in a draw. This can happen in five ways:

[1] players agree that there aren't enough pieces left on the board for either to win;

[2] a player is not in check but is unable to make a legal move (this is called "stalemate");

[3] each player makes fifty moves without any pieces being taken and no pawns being moved. The player making his fiftieth move must declare a draw or the game continues;

[4] the same board position has been repeated three times in a row;

[5] when a player can check an opponent continually in an endless loop, with the king alternating between the same two or more squares.

Touch it, move it

If you touch a piece, you are expected to move it, unless that move is illegal. So think before you touch.

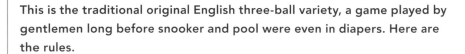
This is the traditional original English three-ball variety, a game played by gentlemen long before snooker and pool were even in diapers. Here are the rules.

It can be played with two or more people. The table is the same as a snooker table, but you only have three balls.

There are two white balls. One has a little black spot on it and the other is just plain white. One player uses the white ball as the cue ball and the other player uses only the white ball with the spot. The third ball is red.

Starting position

At the start of the game, the red is placed on the spot furthest from the "D" (the black spot in snooker, called "the spot"). The first player plays from in-hand, from within the "D," and the second white ball stays off the table until the second player makes his first shot (also in-hand within the "D").

Scoring

Players score as follows:

[1] Potting the opponent's cue ball scores two points. It then stays off the table until the opponent's turn (it is advisable to keep it on the table to enable higher scoring).

[2] Going in-off. This means bouncing your cue ball off another ball, so that your cue ball ends up in a pocket. If you go in-off the red, you score three points. If you go in-off the other white, you score two points.

[3] Cannon. You hit your cue ball and it hits the red and then the red hits the other white (or you hit the white and then it hits the red). This scores two points.

[4] Potting the red scores three points.

If you get a combination of scores with the same shot (e.g., a cannon and an in-off), tote them all up. A player keeps on going until he or she doesn't score.

When the red is potted it returns to the spot. If this is occupied, it goes on the pyramid spot; if the pyramid spot is occupied, it goes on the center spot.

All foul shots score two points for your opponent. A foul shot means that you end your turn and lose all points scored during it. After a foul the other player can play the balls where they are, or move the red to the spot, place your ball onto the center spot, and play his or her own white ball from in-hand from the "D."

High-scoring Tricks

Breaks can get into the thousands.

If you get the two balls very near a pocket it means you can play repeated cannons and in-offs easily.

The ideal thing to do is get the two balls jammed in the pockets so you can get consecutive cannons (but you can't take more than seventy-five consecutive cannons in one turn). And consecutive pots or in-offs not combined with a cannon are restricted to fifteen.

The art of the game is either getting the balls close to the pockets or getting good angles. Angles are very important. You are generally not hitting the balls very hard but are doing gentle strokes most of the time.

Juggling really is easy when you get the knack of it. Like riding a bike, once your body has understood how to do it, it is a skill that you will never forget. Keep practicing the steps below and don't be disheartened if you don't juggle perfectly right away. Even expert jugglers started by dropping a lot of balls.

Juggle With One Ball

Hold the ball in your right hand at about waist level. Throw it in the air so that it travels in an arc whose top is at eye height and catch it in your left hand. Then throw it in an arc to your right hand. Practice until you can throw in the same sized arc every time.

Juggle With Two Balls

Hold a ball in each hand. Throw one ball in your right hand in an arc. When it reaches the top of the arc throw the ball in your left hand. Then catch the first ball with your left hand and the second ball with your right hand. Practice until you can throw in the same sized arc every time, catch every time, and start with your left hand as well as your right.

Juggle With Three Balls

Start with two balls in your right hand and one in your left. Throw the first ball with your right hand, then throw the second ball with your left hand when the first ball has reached the top of its arc. Immediately catch the first ball with your left hand; throw the third ball with your right hand and immediately catch the second ball with the same hand, and so on. Concentrate on throwing rather than catching, as this is the part that is most easily forgotten (you end up holding too many balls).

Common Mistakes

Many novice jugglers find that they throw the ball forward instead of upward, and they keep walking forward to compensate. Stand facing a wall to remind yourself to throw the ball upward and to prevent you from traveling forward.

Keep your hands about waist height; do not bring them up to snatch at the balls—wait for the balls to reach your hands. Always concentrate on throwing in the same even arc at eye level.

If you get stuck, go back a step until you have mastered throwing and catching one or two balls.

Practice over a table or bed and you won't have to bend down so far to pick up your balls.

A simple paper airplane is a classic toy that will provide great fun for adults and children alike. Once you have mastered the art of its construction, you can get more ambitious and decorate your paper before you fold it.

[1] Start with a sheet of paper 8-1/2 by 11 inches in size.

[2] Make a vertical fold down the center of the paper, bringing the left-hand long edge to meet the right-hand edge.

[3] Crease the fold carefully and open up the paper again.

[4] Turn the paper over and repeat steps 2 and 3. Now you should have a strong crease down the middle of the sheet.

[5] Bring the top left-hand corner of the sheet over to meet the centerfold. Make a crease.

[6] Repeat step 5 with the right-hand corner.

[7] The sheet should now form a triangle at the top.

[8] Fold the triangle down so that its point meets the centerfold, making sure the vertical fold you create is at the point where the folds made in steps 5 and 6 end.

[9] You should be left with a sheet with a rectangular shape as the triangle is now inverted, its point facing downward.

[10] Keeping the triangle on the top of the paper, make a vertical fold, bringing the left- and right-hand edges together at the back of the sheet, along the centerfold.

[11] Cut a neat L-shaped corner out of the outside edge of the folded ends.

[12] Open the paper again, with the folded triangle at the top and front.

[13] Repeat steps 5 and 6.

[14] The tip of the downward facing triangle is just visible beneath the notched-out ends of the new upper triangle. Fold the tip back over the notched ends so that it holds these folds in place.

[15] Repeat step 10 so that the sheet is once again folded along the center-fold, its triangular sections on top.

[16] Turn the sheet ninety degrees, so that the pointed tip is on the right.

[17] Fold down the square corner on the left-hand side to make a wing. Be sure to start the fold exactly midway between the sides of the pointed tip, folding the side panel in half.

[18] Turn the sheet over and fold down the remaining square corner to make the other wing.

[19] Your paper airplane is now ready for take-off!

Drawing a realistic horse need not be a difficult task.

Creating A Template

[1] Begin by outlining a basic template of the shape of a horse in pencil. Roughly sketch a square that will give you the height and breadth of the back and body.

[2] At the top two corners of this square, add two ovals. The oval on the right-hand side should be sloped so that the bottom of it leans out to the right, while the top leans out to the left.

[3] Next, draw the neck and head. Draw an elongated triangle with its base sloping across the left-hand oval, and its point up and out to the far left of the square.

[4] Add a circle, nestling under the tip of the triangle for the horse's cheek.

[5] A small square, with its top right-hand corner pointing to the southwest point of the circle's edge, will give you the basic shape for the muzzle at the end of the head.

[6] The legs can be outlined with two straight lines for the front legs, which should show a gentle incline backward, and two slightly bent lines for the hind-legs. These slope gently backward to the hip, then vertically downward from the knee.

[7] The two joints on each leg should be sketched in with small circles for the hips and knees. Add small triangular hooves at the end of two forward sloping short lines.

Fleshing It Out

[1] Begin with the head, linking the square nose to the cheek and adding triangles for ears that point forward.

[2] The neck is currently made from straight sloping lines. These need to arch out on the top. Add a small curve that connects the head and neck underneath.

[3] Next, work on the body, linking the ovals top and bottom. Both lines should curve in toward the body slightly.

[4] Finally draw the legs, adding lines outside the stick legs. Use a triangle with the pointed end facing downward as the thigh on the hind leg.

Bringing It To Life

[1] Add small details: the eye, mouth, nostril, mane, and tail.

[2] Work on the outline, making it run smoothly. Complete the hooves, cutting the back point of the triangle off with a straight line and making the line that outlines the hind-hip curve into the body of the horse slightly.

[3] Clean up the sketch by erasing your template.

Knitting uses interconnecting loops of wool to make fabric.

Getting Started

[1] You will need two knitting needles, size 8 (fourteen-inches long), worsted-weight wool, a large-eyed yarn needle, and some scissors.

[2] Your first step is to make a slipknot on one needle. Fold the wool over to make a looped loose knot and push the needle under one length and through the center of the loop. Tighten the wool around it.

[3] Next, create your first row of stitches, which is called "casting on."

[4] Put the needle with the slipknot into your left hand. Hold the loose yarn in your right hand. Put the right needle into the slipknot from the front to the back of the loop, and slip the point of the needle under the point of the left needle.

[5] Hold both needles in your left hand and bring the yarn from the ball under and over the point of the right needle.

[6] Holding the right needle in your right hand again, pull the yarn through the stitch with the tip of the right needle.

[7] Push the left tip into the back of the new stitch and remove the right needle altogether.

[8] Increase the tension of the stitch by gently pulling on the yarn.

[9] Push the tip of the right needle into the new stitch from the front to the back and under the tip of the left needle.

[10] Repeat steps 5 to 9 until you have made a row of twenty-eight stitches.

Basic Knitting

[1] The needle with the stitches should be in your left hand.

[2] Push the tip of the right needle into the first stitch, from the front to the back as before.

[3] Taking the length of yarn in your right hand, bring it under and over the tip of the right needle.

[4] Gently pull the yarn through the loop of the stitch with the tip of the right needle.

[5] Now that you have made a new stitch, gently slide it off the left needle and onto the right.

[6] Repeat until you have made twenty-eight new stitches onto the right-hand needle.

[7] Make sure you have the tension even throughout. The rows should be about seven-inches wide.

[8] When you wish to start row three, reverse your needles so that the needle without any stitches is now in your right hand again. Continue as before.

Binding Off

When you have created a block of knitting roughly seven- to nine-inches long, you need to remove it from the needles in a process known as "binding off."

[1] Knit two stitches.

[2] Push the left needle into the first of these two stitches and pull it over the second stitch and off the needle.

[3] Knit another stitch, then pull the previous stitch over and off as before.

[4] Continue until there's only one stitch left.

[5] Cut the yarn free from the ball, leaving about six inches.

[6] Thread the end onto the yarn needle and in and out of several stitches to secure it.

READ MUSIC SCALES

Reading music involves learning to crack another written code, in the same way that you learned to read letters and numerals as a child.

The notes are written across a series of five lines known as a stave.

Notes For The Right Hand

When looking at music written for the right hand on a keyboard, the stave starts with a swirly symbol that trails a tail beneath. This is known as the treble clef. Notes on the treble clef are as follows.

Starting from the top line, the notes that sit across a line are:

F

D

B

G

E

An easy phrase will help you remember this (read from the bottom up):

Fruit

Deserves

Boy

Good

Every

In between the lines, four additional notes nestle in the spaces. These are:

E

C

A

F

An easy way to remember these notes is to read them as the word "face" from the bottom up.

Notes For The Left Hand

When music has been written for the left hand on a keyboard, the symbol at the beginning of the stave resembles a backward-facing capital C, with two small dots to the right of it.

The notes that sit across each line are:

A

F

D

B

G

This can also be remembered with an easily remembered phrase (read from the bottom up):

Always

Fruit

Deserve

Boys

Good

The Notes In Between The Lines Read:

G

E

C

A

There is another phrase that will help you remember these notes (read from the bottom up):

Grass

Eat

Cows

All

Understanding The Notes

The notes themselves appear in various forms. The three main types are:

Crotchet

An oval black note, with a tail or stalk, and its center filled in; should be played for one beat.

Minim

An oval note, with a tail or a stalk, and a white center; should be played for two beats.

Semibreve

An oval note, with no tail or stalk, and a white center should be played for four beats.

A note that is immediately followed by a dot needs to be played for half as many beats again. Thus a dotted minim should be played for three counts.

Beats To A Bar

Music on the page appears "boxed in." Each box contains a variety of notes that add up to the same number of beats. The top of the two numerals next to the treble or bass clef symbol tells you how many beats will be in each box.

SING AT A KARAOKE BAR

The popular Japanese pastime has now swept much of the globe and is enjoyed everywhere. But for karaoke first-timers, you will need to acquaint yourself with basic karaoke etiquette.

[1] When you arrive at the bar, take a look through the DJ's song list and select the song you would most like to sing.

[2] Choose your first song very carefully. Although talent is not important in a karaoke bar, if you select a song that is too ambitious for your debut performance, you are more likely to be overcome by nerves.

[3] Think about the range of notes in the song (how high and how low the tune goes). This can add to the difficulty of a song and to your stress level.

[4] Once you have chosen your song, write the details down on a piece of paper and hand it to the DJ.

[5] You may decide you would like to rehearse a few songs before your stage debut. This can be easily done either using the many karaoke websites, or by purchasing a karaoke CD.

[6] When it is your turn to sing, the DJ will call you up on stage.

[7] The backing instrumental music will be played, and you will be provided with the lyrics to sing into the microphone.

[8] Don't sing too close to the microphone as your voice will be distorted and it will spoil your performance.

[9] Do not hassle the DJ if you feel he or she has not called you up in time. Some DJs prefer to call out similar types of song in sessions, rather than on a first-come-first-served basis.

[10] Do not be put off if you are labeled a "karaoke virgin." It is simply a cue to the audience that they should expect you to feel (and possibly act) a little nervous.

[11] Karaoke audiences are typically a generous crowd the world over. Applaud every performance. It is never OK to boo a singer.

[12] Many karaoke bars are frequented by a variety of people. Some are just out to have a bit of fun, whereas others are serious singers. Don't feel intimidated if you come across a confident singer with a great voice. Karaoke is about the joining in, regardless of your voice.

[13] If you go on stage as part of a crowd, be careful not to pull at the microphone.

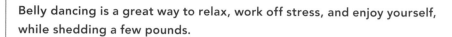

BELLY DANCE

Belly dancing is a great way to relax, work off stress, and enjoy yourself, while shedding a few pounds.

Before You Begin

[1] The easiest way to learn is to sign up for a local class.

[2] You will need to find some comfortable clothes for dancing. Loose skirts or pants are ideal. Tie a scarf around your hips so that you can see that area easily. Wearing a leotard or a body-stocking with this will be ideal.

Warm Up First

As with any exercise, you need to warm up gradually before you begin. The warm-up should prepare your body for the movements that are to follow; therefore, you will need to isolate and rotate each part of your body in turn.

Shake yourself down and begin to rotate your feet, one leg at a time. Move these rotations up through your knees, then to your whole leg. Now rotate your hips, trunk, shoulders, and neck in turn. Do these movements slowly and graciously. Do not strain. Do some gentle stretches and finish with another shake-down.

How To Stand

The way you stand and hold your body is an essential part of the belly dance. Stand with your feet at hip's width and pointing straight forward. Do not lock your legs at the knee.

Keep your head and neck stretched up at all times, and make sure your chin is neither tucked in or jutting upward. Keep your knees and hands loose and relaxed. Indeed, loosening the knees and paying careful attention not to lock them throughout the dance frees up a lot of movement in your hips.

How To Move

One of the basic movements that you can begin to work on at home is to rotate your hips.

[1] Loosen your knees and ensure that your feet are in line with your hips.

[2] Pull your head and neck up tall, keeping your upper body as upright as possible throughout.

[3] Keeping your feet and torso as still as possible, slowly begin to rotate your hips. Keep the movement in your legs from the ankles and knees.

[4] "Draw" a clockwise circle with your hips. When you have built up a momentum in this direction, reverse the circle.

[5] Keep the circles compact at first.

[6] Now begin to turn into your hip circles. Lifting one foot at a time, just a tiny way off the floor, gradually turn your body in the direction of your hip circles.

This move can be developed further with circular arm movements or shimmies with your shoulders.

DANCE THE WALTZ

If you want to take up ballroom dancing, the waltz is a good place to start. It is smooth and romantic and relatively easy to master.

The waltz is a dance of Austrian peasant origin in 3/4 time, which means there are three equal beats to the measure and about thirty-two measures per minute. In its early history it was the subject of much controversy, since the close face-to-face position was considered too physically intimate, leading to it being banned as immoral in some places for years.

[1] The man holds the woman by placing his right hand beneath her left arm. He extends his left arm to hold her right hand. The woman places her left hand on the man's right shoulder to form the basic waltz position, known as the "closed position."

[2] Usually, the man leads the woman in one of four basic directions, and the woman follows. He signals which way the woman should move by his hand position and pressure.

[3] To move to the left, he pushes to the left with his left hand. To move to the right he pulls the woman gently to the right with his right hand. To move forward (backward for the woman), the man pushes her gently backward with the right hand and extends his left hand; to move backward (forward for the woman) he pulls her toward him gently with his right hand while drawing his left hand in.

[4] While the man signals his intentions with his upper body, the feet of both dancers move in sync; every step the man takes, the woman does in reverse.

[5] The simplest waltz foot movement is called the box step, as the dancers move in a square (or box). The man takes one step forward with the left foot, then slides his other foot to meet it; then he takes two steps to the side and slides the other foot to resume the closed position; this is followed by one step backward with the right foot and he resumes the closed position by sliding the left foot; finally he takes two steps to the side and resumes the closed position by sliding the other foot, so the dancers end up where they started.

[6] The step-slide . . . step-step-slide . . . motion should be smooth and grace-ful. After much practice the partnership becomes instinctive, as both dancers trust each other, gain in confidence, and communicate efficiently.

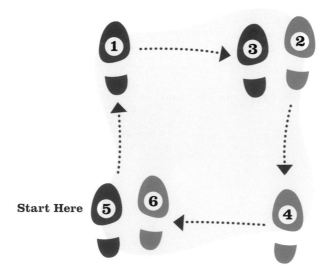

Start Here

DO A CARTWHEEL

Whether you want to be a cheerleader, or impress your grandchildren, a cartwheel is a relatively simple, though impressive, gymnastic maneuver. Here are instructions for a right-handed cartwheel. If you are left-handed, simply reverse them.

[1] Stand sideways to the direction you want to travel, with both arms raised in the air, close to your ears, with your right side at the front, and your right foot pointing forward.

[2] During the cartwheel your body will rotate 360 degrees as you keep your body on the same plane, rolling forwards in a star jump.

[3] You will make contact with the ground like this: right foot, right hand, left hand, left foot, right foot (although for the sake of rhythm and memory, just think "hand, hand, foot, foot").

[4] Most of your weight is in your back (left) leg. Bend your right leg and transfer your body weight into it. This will tip you forward and off balance. Now there's no going back!

[5] Reach forward with your right arm straight, palm flat, and fingers facing to the right (perpendicular to your foot). At the same, time kick your left leg up straight. Don't bend at the waist, or your star shape will collapse and your legs will travel sideways rather than vertically.

[6] As soon as your right hand makes firm contact with the ground, your right foot should leave the ground, so that for a moment only your right hand is in contact with the floor.

[7] Immediately place your left hand on the ground, about shoulder width in front of your right.

[8] Bring your right hand off the floor and land with your left foot facing the direction you have just come from.

[9] Land your right foot on the floor and regain your balance so that your weight is evenly spread between your two feet.

The best way to ensure healthy teeth and gums and fresh breath is to brush your teeth routinely. Though this will come as no surprise, careless dental hygiene is very common.

When To Brush

Ideally you should brush three times a day: after breakfast, at lunch, and last thing at night. Keep a toothbrush at the office and try to remember to brush after lunch, even if it is without toothpaste. Brushing just before bedtime is crucial, otherwise the bacteria responsible for tooth decay will thrive overnight.

Choosing A Toothbrush

Always choose toothbrushes made with synthetic fibers, as bacteria can lurk within the porous fibers of natural bristles. The head of your toothbrush should be small: an inch long at most. Many modern brushes are equipped with a dye that will fade once it is time to replace the brush. You will need to buy a new brush every three months, or whenever the bristles are frayed. Bacteria can thrive on a toothbrush between brushes, so you should also replace your toothbrush after a cold or a sore throat, because the bacteria on your brush can cause reinfection.

How To Store Your Toothbrush

Don't disinfect your brush after use, as there is little evidence to support the benefit of doing so. Rinse your toothbrush in tap water and store it upright and exposed to the air. Avoid storing it inside a container, as the warm, humid air will serve as a breeding ground for bacteria. If the family's brushes are all stored together, it is vital that they are not all in contact, as oral infections such as gingivitis can be spread in this way. Consider storing your brushes away from the toilet: scientific studies have identified *E. coli* on brushes exposed to airborne droplets from flushing.

How To Brush

[1] Use a small amount of fluoridated toothpaste.

[2] Hold the brush at a forty-five-degree angle to your teeth, so that the bristles clean under the gum.

[3] Brush in either a circular or an elliptical motion, sweeping the teeth from the gum to the edge of each tooth.

[4] Focus on brushing a small number of teeth at once.

[5] Remember to brush three sides of each tooth: front, back, and chewing surface.

[6] Take your time! Use a timer and spend two to three minutes brushing.

[7] Brush the surface of the tongue carefully—this will remove the bacteria that can cause bad breath.

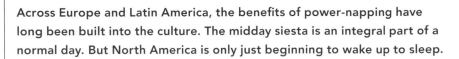

TAKE A POWER-NAP

Across Europe and Latin America, the benefits of power-napping have long been built into the culture. The midday siesta is an integral part of a normal day. But North America is only just beginning to wake up to sleep.

Why Take A Power-Nap?

Many studies indicate that most Americans are not getting enough sleep. It is estimated that many of us are deprived of about an hour's-worth a day, with parents of newborn infants clocking hundreds of hours of lost sleep in the first year.

Taking daily naps of twenty or thirty minutes will top-off your body's essential sleep, and has been proven to increase your ability to concentrate, learn new information, and make crucial decisions.

What Are The Health Benefits Of Power-Napping?

Sleep deprivation will not only affect your concentration and decision-making capabilities; it has also been linked to an increased tendency for obesity, as a tired body craves more sugary and fatty foods. In addition, it has been shown that regular power-napping can considerably reduce your risk of heart disease and stroke.

When Is The Best Time To Take A Nap?

The optimum time to take a power-nap is eight hours after you first wake in the morning. More generally, between the hours of 1 P.M. and 3 P.M. seems to be the most effective. Twenty minutes taken at this time leaves you feeling considerably more refreshed than an extra twenty minutes during the night. If you are anticipating a late night at the office, or socially, and know that you will not get a good night's sleep, take a nap in advance. It will be more valuable than waiting to catch up the following day.

How Should You Nap?

[1] Make yourself comfortable. Loosen your clothing at the collar and re-move your shoes.

[2] If you can close the blinds or the drapes, do so. Lock the door and turn off the phone.

[3] Set an alarm for a half-hour's time: any longer than that and you will feel groggy when you wake up.

[4] Stretch out on a sofa or sit back in an armchair with your feet up, if you can. Otherwise, rest your head in your arms on the desk.

[5] Breathe deeply and picture yourself somewhere relaxing: the beach, a hammock, or simply in your own bed.

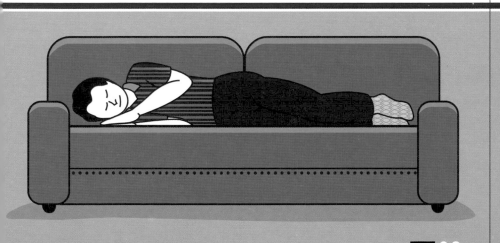

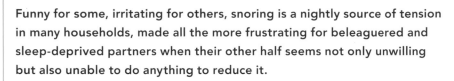

REDUCE SNORING

Funny for some, irritating for others, snoring is a nightly source of tension in many households, made all the more frustrating for beleaguered and sleep-deprived partners when their other half seems not only unwilling but also unable to do anything to reduce it.

What Causes Snoring?

Snoring is caused by the vibrating of tissue (often the soft palate and uvula—the fleshy thing that hangs down in the back of your throat) in a restricted airway.

Ten Steps To Snore-free Sleeping

[1] Losing weight can make a dramatic impact on snoring, as it helps to reduce the size of the soft palate at the back of the roof of the mouth and improves breathing by reducing fatty tissue in the affected areas. Often, this single factor alone is responsible for the majority of snoring problems.

[2] Avoid drinking alcohol before going to sleep. This increases muscle relaxation, makes the nasal passages more constricted, and may be responsible for some of your excess weight.

[3] Many snorers sleep on their backs. Sleeping on your side often reduces snoring. Some snorers even go as far as taping a tennis ball to their back to prevent them from lying on it.

[4] If you must sleep on your back, prop yourself up a little with pillows so your upper body is slightly inclined.

[5] Smoking is thought to disrupt sleep and contribute to snoring. Kick the habit and you'll not only live longer, you'll sleep longer too.

[6] Sleeping with the mouth open is also thought to cause snoring. Use a chinstrap to keep your mouth closed, and use a nasal strip to increase the airflow through your nose.

[7] Take up a hobby that uses your voice, such as singing. This will retrain and tone-up weak muscles in your throat.

[8] In some cases a tense jaw may contribute to snoring. Before going to sleep, place your hands on the side of your jaw. Drawing them downward twenty times while pressing gently against your open jaw will help to reduce some of the tension that builds up during the day. Avoid chewing gum, which makes the jaw very tense and tired.

[9] Use your vacuum cleaner more frequently in the bedroom. Allergies to dust and airborne particles may be affecting your breathing.

[10] If none of the above works, it may be time to visit your doctor and ask about using a C-PAP (continuous positive airway pressure) machine. You may have a serious medical condition called sleep apnea.

BEHAVE IN A RESTAURANT

If you know how to conduct yourself in a restaurant, not only will you and those around you have a more comfortable and enjoyable experience, the restaurant staff will actually give you better service.

[1] Confirm your reservation before you arrive, and show up on time. If you are late, don't be surprised if you have to wait for another table. Call ahead if you are going to be more than fifteen minutes late.

[2] Dress up rather than down; it is better to be overdressed than under-dressed. Act confident, but not arrogant. You must look like the sort of person who expects to receive good service; if you look like a bum, what do you think your chances will be? You're also more likely to be given better seats at a prominent table. If the restaurant requires that you wear a jacket, keep it on.

[3] If you are meeting a date, do so before you arrive at the restaurant, otherwise one of you may have to sit alone waiting for the other to arrive.

[4] Wait for everyone at the table to be served before you begin eating. If there is a host, wait for that person to begin eating first.

[5] Do not place your cell phone on the table. Keep it out of sight and either switched off, or set to vibrate.

[6] Communicate effectively with the waiter or waitress. That means treating him or her with respect, rather than as a lackey. People who feel uncomfortable in restaurants often overcompensate and are overly stern and dismissive with the waiter, because they feel that they, the customer, should be higher in status and somehow "in control." Smile, look them in the eye and treat them with respect, and you'll get the service you deserve.

[7] Control your children. Noisy and disruptive offspring not only lessen your enjoyment, they also disturb the other diners. If you can't keep your children under control, leave them at home with a babysitter. Keep your own noise levels down, too, especially if you are with a celebrating group.

[8] If you have found your meal especially enjoyable, send your compliments to the chef—he or she will appreciate good feedback.

[9] An acceptable tip for excellent service should be in the range of 15 to 20 percent. If the food is unpalatable, do not penalize the waiters by skimping on the tip—they don't cook it.

Across the U.S., tipping is no longer considered optional. Good service should always be rewarded with a tip; poor service, it seems, should be rewarded with a less generous tip, never with nothing at all. The only exception to this is where a coffee shop has a tip jar at the counter. With any self-service restaurant, the tip jar should be seen as entirely optional.

Tipping At Restaurants

The Maitre d':
If a kindly Maitre d' has led you to a table, despite your having no reservation and it being a busy night, you should probably think of tipping around $20

The Waiters:
For good service, 15 to 20 percent of the check
For poor service, 10 percent

The Wine Waiter:
Around 15 percent of the cost of the bottle

The Parking Valet:
$2 for parking and retrieving your car

The Bartender:
At least $1 per alcoholic drink, up to 15 percent of the check

Tipping On Vacation

The Taxi Driver:
10 to 15 percent of the cost of the fare

$1 PER BAG

The Skycap At The Airport:
$1 to $2 per bag, depending on whether or not your bags are taken to the check-in counter

Hotel Doorman:
$1 for a cab, more if he helps with your luggage

Hotel Bellhop:
$1 per bag, especially if he takes your bag to your room

Hotel Housekeeper:
At least $2 per night spent at the hotel

Room Service Personnel:
15 percent of the check

Tour Guide:
$2 to $5 per two hours of tour

Cruise Ship Cabin Stewards:
$3 per guest per day at the end of your stay

Cruise Ship Maitre d':
At least $10 per week of your cruise, or $2 per guest per day at the end of your stay

Casino Cocktail Waitress:
$1 to $5 per round of drinks

Casino Dealers:
Anything from $2 to $100 per bet, during play, depending on how flush you are feeling!

Casino Change People and Keno Runners:
$1 to $25 during play

Holiday Season Tipping

The Children's Schoolteacher:
A small gift

Au Pair Or Nanny:
One-week's to one-month's pay and a small gift

Babysitter:

An evening's pay

Mail Carrier:

Gifts under $20

Newspaper Deliverer:

$10 to $30

Trash/Recycling Collectors:

$10 to $20 each

Apartment Doormen:

$20 to $100

Everyday Tipping

Pizza Delivery Personnel:

10 percent of your check

Furniture Deliverers:

$10 each

Hair Stylist, Including The Salon Owner:

15 to 20 percent of the bill

Manicurist/Pedicurist:

15 percent of the bill

Barber:

15 to 20 percent

On a busy Friday night in the center of town, a decent bar may be crowded with people waiting to get served. So what can you do to cut your waiting time?

Where people go wrong

[1] Take a look in the far corner of the bar, where the crowd is thinnest. That would be the best place to go stand, right? Wrong. There's usually a pretty good reason why few people are waiting there. See the two portly and seasoned beer drinkers who have positioned themselves on the stools there? No one's getting past these two in a hurry. Pick a different spot.

[2] The guys at the bar who beckon and heckle the bartender are sure to be the last ones to get served. Whistle, call out what you guess may be the bartender's name, or snap your fingers repeatedly, calling, "Hey, what's it take to get a drink around here?" and you may need to settle in for a long wait.

[3] Have a complicated and time-consuming order and the bartender will remember your face the next time you come to get a round of drinks and avoid you. Just as frustrating on a busy night is the customer who lists an order in staggered stages so that the bartender has to make several trips back to the bar to piece the order together.

[4] Another thing that is sure to get your face noticed is being unprepared. The guy who doesn't have his money ready, who hasn't yet decided on what he's having, or who has forgotten half the order and keeps the bartender waiting is sure to be avoided the next time around.

How to get it right

So how do you get noticed and get served as quickly as possible?

[1] First, you are going to have to carry out some very careful maneuvering to get yourself close enough to the bar to make eye contact with the bartender.

[2] Stay calm! You are far more likely to be served before the hecklers if you remain polite at all times.

[3] Establish eye contact with the bartender and smile.

[4] Know exactly what you are ordering, and give your order clearly so that he or she gets it the first time.

[5] Tip well. A generous tipper will be served promptly the next time around.

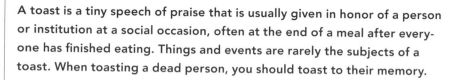

PROPOSE A TOAST

A toast is a tiny speech of praise that is usually given in honor of a person or institution at a social occasion, often at the end of a meal after everyone has finished eating. Things and events are rarely the subjects of a toast. When toasting a dead person, you should toast to their memory.

[1] Stand up in a prominent place and get everyone's attention.

[2] Wait a few moments until the room is silent. Then hold your glass in front of you, just above waist level, while you speak.

[3] Begin by saying "I would like to propose a toast . . ." Speak slowly and clearly and keep your words brief and heartfelt. Some of the most touching toasts are simple, personal, and uniquely suited to the occasion. About four or five sentences lasting no longer than a minute is usually adequate.

[4] As you speak, look at the person being honored, from time to time. Remember that the toast is about them, not you.

[5] Your words should appeal and relate to everyone in the group. So make sure that the tone and content are appropriate; your grandmother may not have the same sense of humor as your drinking buddies.

[6] This is an opportunity to say kind words, not humiliate or embarrass. Also, avoid in-jokes. If it is a small, intimate group, then everyone may well know what you are talking about, but if you are toasting someone in a room full of relative strangers, keep your references at a level that everyone can understand so that nobody feels excluded.

[7] Conclude your toast by raising your glass to eye level and inviting the as-

sembled guests to toast in honor of the individual. Ask everyone, except the person you are toasting, to rise and fill their glasses.

[8] This is done by expressing hope for the future. For example, "May his/her success continue . . . May s/he have as much fun in the next job as s/he has had in this one . . ." and then end by saying "To . . ." and say the name of the person being toasted.

[9] The audience may repeat your last phrase, then everyone takes a drink and sits down again.

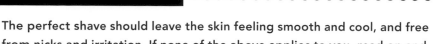

The perfect shave should leave the skin feeling smooth and cool, and free from nicks and irritation. If none of the above applies to you, read on and consider changing your shaving habits.

[1] Forget electric razors. They lacerate the skin at the microscopic level. The best shave is a wet shave.

[2] Wet shave: the clue is in the name. Some men actually apply shaving cream or gel to a dry face. Wet your face with hot water before applying the foam or gel. Better yet, shave directly after taking a bath or shower. Your whiskers will be hydrated, and therefore softer and easier to cut.

[3] The choice of foam is crucial. Most men use gels and foams from a can, but the best shave is achieved using good-quality glycerin-based shaving cream from a tub and investing in a genuine badger-hair shaving brush (which start at about $50 and can cost up to ten times as much).

[4] Allow the brush to soak in the basin while you fill it with hot water. Hold the brush bristle downward to allow the excess water to drain, then dip the end into your tub of cream and lather it onto your face.

[5] A shaving brush serves two important functions. First, it gives you a much richer hydrating lather than is possible by using your hands; and second, the bristles exfoliate your skin and make the whiskers stand out, so they can be cut more easily.

[6] If you must use disposable razors, purchase some average-priced ones with one or two blades. Don't bother with the fancy three- or four-blade disposables that cost a fortune. The best razor of all is the old-fashioned double-edge adjustable razor, because the blade is of better quality and sharper. Also, since the razor is heavier you don't have to use any pressure at all, so it is kinder on your skin.

[7] Simply draw the razor down your face along its contours. Modern disposable razors require more pressure and irritate the skin, unlike a double-edge razor. If you suffer from razor-burn and sore skin, a few weeks with a double-edge razor and shaving cream will change that.

[8] After you have finished shaving, rinse your face and neck with hot water (or apply a hot damp towel), and then splash with cold water to close the pores.

[9] Apply an alcohol-free aftershave or moisturizer.

[10] Rinse the shaving brush and store with the bristles upright, so they dry without being damaged.

There's nothing worse than stepping into a salon with high expectations only to emerge thirty minutes later fighting the urge to walk straight to the nearest hat shop. A bad haircut will stay with you for six weeks or more and can easily be avoided with a few basic precautions.

Know Your Own Face

Examine your face carefully in the mirror. Decide whether it is heart-shaped, round, oval, or square. Different face shapes will only look their best with certain styles. Choose carelessly and you may emerge disappointed.

Examine Famous Faces

Take the time to browse through the photographs of celebrities in a glossy magazine. Draw a circle around those with styles you admire. Now take a closer look at those faces. Does the celebrity have the same face shape as you? What about the texture of the hair? If yours is naturally curly or perfectly straight, you will need to keep that in mind as you select styles sported by celebrities with a similar hair texture.

Examine Friends' Faces

Take a close look at your friends' hair, applying the same principles as above. Ask them where they go to have their hair done, and consider accompanying them to their next appointment. You can take this opportunity to really scrutinize the way in which the stylists work. Which of them are really concentrating, asking their clients the most pertinent questions about their requirements, and producing the most impressive results?

Making The Appointment

Make sure your appointment includes time for a consultation so that you can discuss your needs and your ideas about your style thoroughly. Don't be rushed: you are paying for the stylist's time as well as expertise. Take along photographs of cuts you have selected, or even photographs of yourself sporting a favorite cut.

Communication

Be as precise as you can about your likes and dislikes. If you are prepared to spend time on a daily basis working your hair with styling products, say so. If, like most people, you need a style that will work well on a daily basis with minimal fuss, this is important too. The key is to speak up: be exact about everything you consider to be essential information before the stylist begins to cut. Be prepared to compromise, and listen to any advice your stylist may have: it may be that the cut you envision may not be the most suitable for you.

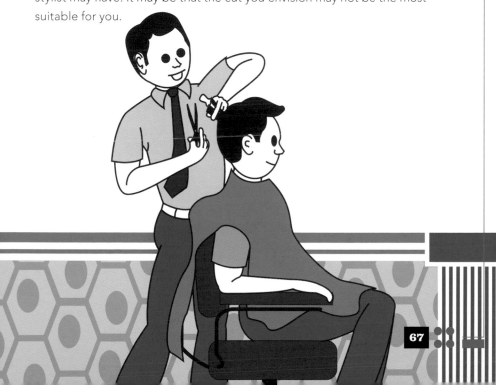

CHOOSE A PAIR OF SUNGLASSES

There's much more to choosing shades than how they look. The most important consideration is how well they protect your eyes from the harmful rays of the sun.

Sun Protection

The quality of the lens is very important. First, it must provide protection against harmful ultraviolet (UV) radiation (both types A and B) from the sun. Only buy shades that provide one hundred percent UVA and UVB protection. Ultraviolet rays can seriously injure your eyes, causing retina and muscle damage, cataracts, and cancer. Cheap lenses with little UV protection are worse than wearing no shades, because the dark lens will cause your iris to open more, allowing even more harmful rays to reach your retina.

Don't be impressed by the darkness of the lens. Dark does not necessarily mean protection, and lighter lenses are kinder on the eyes, since they allow more of the "good" light through.

Look for lenses that filter out some of the sun's blue light. You can tell by looking at the sky, which should appear gray.

Small lenses provide less protection than larger ones. Best of all are wraparound shades that prevent light from leaking in around the sides of your eyes. The top of your eyes and eyelids need protecting too.

Choose glass lenses where possible, since they give the greatest clarity and are more scratch-resistant. If you wear your shades while playing sports choose a lightweight and shatterproof polycarbonate lens, rather than heavier and less durable glass.

Cheap, inferior lenses afford poorer visibility; if you wear them for any length of time, even in the shade, and your eyes will quickly become tired.

Lens Color

Sunglasses are tinted to reduce glare, but the color of the coating has different effects on your vision:

Brown, gray, or green lenses will reduce glare and eyestrain but won't affect your color perception. Yellow or gold lenses are less effective at reducing glare, but they are effective in low-light conditions, and their increased depth perception makes them an excellent choice for snow—skiing or snowboarding. Pink lenses enhance the contrast of objects against blue or green backgrounds and aren't too dark, so they are good for driving. Mirror-shades are useful in very bright conditions (such as high altitudes where the air is thinner) but should not be used in low-light situations, otherwise you won't be able to see very much—they make the world seem very dark.

Follow a few tips and you can always feel confident that you look your best.

The best overall tip for all body types is to stand tall. No one looks their best when they slouch. Try imagining an invisible thread pulling up through the center of your head. This will lift your head and neck, and help to keep your back straight and tall.

Lessening Height

[1] Choose pants with cuffs.

[2] Wear your shirts and tops longer and looser to make your legs look shorter.

[3] Avoid monochromatic outfits: go dark on top and lighter on the bottom, or vice versa.

[4] Never choose vertical stripes.

[5] Don't do delicate! Look for larger detailing on your outfits.

Adding Height

[1] Choose narrow-legged pants that are tailored to fit your behind and thighs.

[2] Wear your tops tucked into your trousers.

[3] Wear vertical stripes.

[4] V-neck tops will add an illusion of height.

[5] Heeled shoes and short skirts will also add height.

Lessening Breadth

[1] Keep your tops open at the neck. Wear V-necks and keep your shirts unbuttoned a little.

[2] Stick to one color on the top and a lighter on the bottom.

[3] Darker colors will slim your appearance.

[4] Sticking to all one color throughout will also slim your appearance.

[5] Bias-cut, lightweight dresses for women, or tuxedo, double-, or single-breasted jackets for men make slimming evening-wear choices.

[6] Wide-legged palazzo pants will flatter your thighs.

[7] Choose a thicker, sturdier fabric for your pants, that will draw everything in a little, rather than silks and thin cotton that will not disguise any jiggle.

The Broad-shouldered

[1] Avoid anything that will attract attention to the contrast between your waist and your shoulders, such as a tightly belted small waist.

[2] Avoid anything that will attract attention to your shoulder area, such as puffed sleeves on women, and padded shoulders on men or women.

[3] Choose soft fabrics that sit easily on the shoulders.

[4] Go for monochromatic outfits, or wear a darker colored top.

[5] Avoid wearing your hair at shoulder-length and go for bright accessories that will draw the eye away from your shoulders.

[6] A pinstripe is a good way to distract attention from broad shoulders.

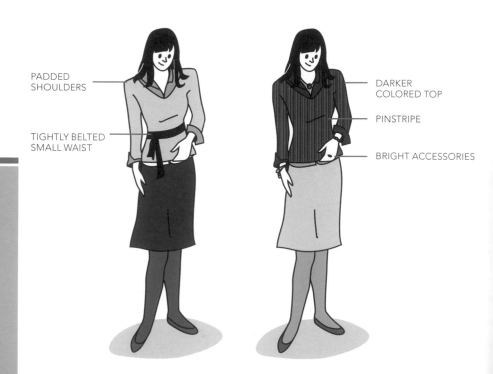

PADDED
SHOULDERS

TIGHTLY BELTED
SMALL WAIST

DARKER
COLORED TOP

PINSTRIPE

BRIGHT ACCESSORIES

International Care Labels were designed to be instantly recognizable in any language.

What The Label Should Tell You

[1] The most appropriate washing method.

[2] The best water temperature.

[3] The safest drying method.

[4] The hottest iron temperature.

What The Symbols Mean

There are five basic symbols.

A washbasin will give you information about how to wash the garment and at what temperature.

A square will give you information about how to dry the garment.

A triangle will tell you whether or not the garment can be treated with bleach.

An iron will give you information about how hot to set the iron.

A circle means that the garment is suitable for dry-cleaning.

Washing

 One dot within the tub indicates the water temperature should be no higher than 85°F. Two dots indicate a temperature of no higher than 105°F; three dots, no more than 120°F; four dots, no more than 140°F.

 One or two bars across the tub indicates that the garments should be washed as delicates.

 A hand in the waves is the symbol for "hand-wash only."

 Do not wash the garment if the washtub has been crossed through.

Drying

 Three vertical lines inside the square indicate that the garment should drip dry.

 A single horizontal line indicates that the garment should be dried flat.

 If the square contains a circle that has been crossed through, the garment should not be dried in a hot air drier.

 If the inner circle contains a dot, the drier should be set to a lower temperature. Three dots in the circle means that the drier can be set at its hottest.

Bleaching

 An empty triangle indicates that the garment is suitable for bleaching.

 If the triangle is crossed with diagonal stripes, you should use a color-safe, non-chlorine bleach.

 A solid triangle that has been crossed through indicates that the garment is not suitable for bleaching.

Dry-Cleaning

 A circle means that the garment must be dry-cleaned.

 A circle with a "P" inside indicates to the dry-cleaner which solvents must not be used.

 A circle that has been crossed through cannot be dry-cleaned.

Ironing

 The number of dots that appear with the iron indicate how hot to set the iron, with one dot for the coolest setting and three for the hottest.

 An iron with a cross beneath it is an indication that the garment is not suitable for steam ironing.

 An empty iron, with no dots, indicates the garment can be ironed at any temperature, with or without steam.

The key to keeping your clothes easily accessible and looking their best, whether in the closet or in the suitcase, is to learn how to fold them correctly.

Fabrics In Your Closet

It is important to establish which of your clothes should be folded and which should be hung in your closet. Always fold woolen garments, as hanging will cause them to lose their shape, particularly at the shoulders. Store any woolens along with blocks of cedar wood or scented herb sachets in order to prevent moth damage. Dress shirts and blouses, formal outfits, suits, and skirts will crease less if they are hung. Likewise, linen, silk, and rayon will also need to be hung.

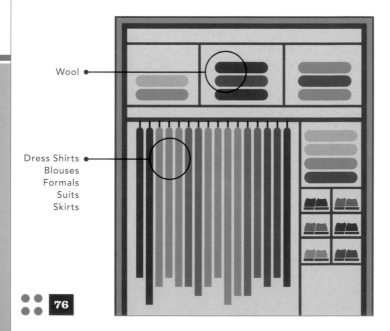

Wool

Dress Shirts
Blouses
Formals
Suits
Skirts

Pants

[1] Lay ironed pants face up on a flat surface.

[2] Smooth them out until they are perfectly crease-free.

[3] Fold one leg across to meet the other, lining up both inner- and outer-edge seams.

[4] Make two horizontal folds: bring the bottom of the pants up as far as the top of the back pocket, and then bring the newly-folded outside edge up to the waistband.

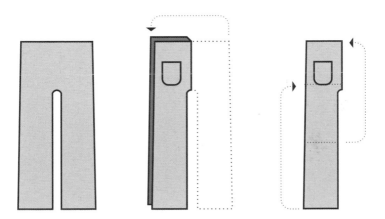

T-shirts

[1] Lay the ironed T-shirt face down on a flat surface.

[2] Smooth it out until it is perfectly crease-free.

[3] Make two vertical folds, bringing the edges in until they line up with the outside edge of the neckband.

[4] Fold each sleeve back to line up with the newly folded outside edge of the T-shirt.

[5] Make a horizontal fold: bring the bottom edge up as far as the sleeves.

[6] Finally, fold again so the bottom fold meets the neckband.

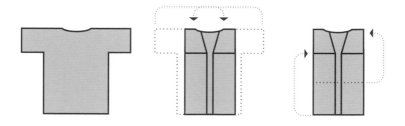

Dress Shirts, Blouses, And Other Long-sleeved Shirts

[1] Lay the ironed shirt face down on a flat surface.

[2] Smooth it out until it is perfectly crease-free.

[3] Fold each sleeve horizontally so that the cuff meets the seam of the opposite shoulder.

[4] Make two vertical folds: bring each side into the middle of the shirt.

[5] Make two horizontal folds: first bringing the bottom up as far as the folded sleeves. Finally, bring this folded edge up to meet the collar.

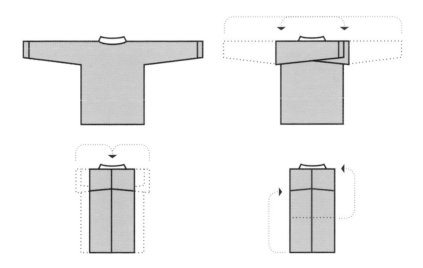

To give your clothes that professional laundered look, teach yourself an ironing routine that will leave them looking crisp and sharp.

Shirt

[1] Read the care label to get the correct ironing temperature (see page 73).

[2] Iron the shirt while it is still a little damp. It is very difficult to remove creases from garments that are bone dry.

[3] Iron the back of the collar first, followed by the front, working in from the edges. Hold the material taut as you iron to prevent puckering.

[4] Open the cuffs and iron them, working in from the edges. Press the inside first, then the outside. Do not make a crease.

[5] Smooth the sleeves flat to avoid creases and iron, once with the seams parallel, and again with one seam on top of the other. Do not make a crease. You want to end up with a smooth cylinder.

[6] Place the shirt face-down on the ironing board and iron from the shoulders (the "yoke") to the shirttail.

[7] Iron the right front panel, pulling it tight along the button line as you press in between the buttons. Then turn it and iron the back, and finally the left front panel.

[8] Place the shirt on a hanger (not wire), do up a few top buttons, and allow it to cool down. Do not wear immediately, or it will quickly become creased again.

Pants

[1] Turn your pants inside out and iron the pockets, waistband, flies, seams, and hems. Turn them right side out again. The top of the pants will now be easier to iron. Wrinkled and bunched-up pockets make ironing very irksome.

[2] Pull the waistband over the top of the board and iron the upper part of the pants, starting on one side and turning them.

[3] Lay the pants along the length of the ironing board with legs and all four seams lined up. Smooth out creases by hand then lift the top leg and fold it back to expose the bottom inside leg. Iron this from hem to crotch and along the existing crease.

[4] Turn the pants over, fold over the top leg, and iron the inside of the other leg.

[5] Place both legs together and iron the upper outside leg, then turn over and iron the second outside leg.

[6] Hang the pants up immediately and allow them to cool before wearing.

Ties are out of fashion in many sectors of the business world, but just because you go to work in jeans and loafers, or an open-collar shirt, there will still be plenty of occasions where knowing how to tie a tie with style and flair will be a must.

Half Windsor

This is your standard thick knot, and it requires a long tie.

[1] Button up your collar and raise it. Drape the tie round your neck with the end of the wide part placed twelve inches below the thin end.

[2] Wrap the thick end over the thin and bring it toward you and down through the loop.

[3] Wrap the thick end from left to right around the triangle which you created in step 2, then bring it up through the loop from behind.

[4] Push the thick end through the knot, then slide the knot up to your top button while holding the thin end.

Full Windsor

This more traditional version of the Half Windsor gives a very thick symmetrical knot.

[1] Button up your collar and raise it. Drape the tie around your neck with the wide part placed twelve inches below the thin end.

[2] Wrap the thick end over the thin, then bring it up through the loop from behind.

[3] Wrap it once around the loop clockwise and bring it up through the loop from behind a second time.

[4] Push the thick end through the knot, then slide the knot up to your top button while holding the thin end.

Pratt Knot

Also known as the Shelby Knot, this gives a tidy knot, that is slightly less wide than the Windsor.

[1] Button up your collar and raise it. Drape the tie inside out around your neck with the thin part in front of the thick.

[2] Bring the thick end toward you and pass it through the loop, then pull it downward and tighten it.

[3] Bring the wide end around the front from right to left and pass it through the loop from behind.

[4] Push the thick end through the knot, then slide the knot up to your top button while holding the thin end.

HALF WINDSOR   FULL WINDSOR   PRATT KNOT

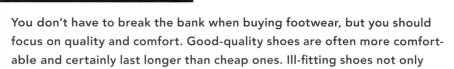

CHOOSE SHOES

You don't have to break the bank when buying footwear, but you should focus on quality and comfort. Good-quality shoes are often more comfortable and certainly last longer than cheap ones. Ill-fitting shoes not only damage your feet, they affect your whole body posture.

Comfort

[1] Children should always get their feet measured before fitting, and adults should also get measured from time to time, as many of them go for decades assuming they are a certain size (one in six Americans are walking around in shoes that fit poorly). Fit at the end of the day when your feet are largest. Choose shoes for their fit, not for the size you think you are.

[2] Wear the appropriate thickness of socks. For example, don't shop for dress shoes while wearing thick sports socks.

[3] Press on the front of the shoe to find your big toe. There should be a thumb's width between your toe and the front of the shoe.

[4] The foot should not move from side to side inside the shoe (if it does, choose a thinner width) and the side of your foot should not stick out over the sole (if it does, choose a wider width).

[5] Walk around while wearing the shoes. If shoes don't feel comfortable, don't buy them and don't rely on breaking them in. Tight shoes will not loosen and stretch sufficiently to fit. Good quality, well-fitted shoes should be comfortable immediately and should not rub anywhere or scrape against the ankle bone.

[6] When buying athletic shoes, make sure you match the shoe to the activity. Different sports require different weights, soles, lacing patterns, and cushioning. For example, a basketball shoe has a wide rubber sole to grip the floor and has lots of lateral stability, whereas a jogging shoe is very light, with lots of cushioning in the sole, but provides little lateral support.

Quality

[1] Examine the shoe to check for irregularities—frayed seams, gaps between shoe and sole, etc. On good shoes, the soles are glued and stitched to the uppers.

[2] Leather shoes are preferable to those made of synthetic materials because leather allows the foot to breathe, adapts to the shape of the foot, and is durable.

[3] The interior is just as important as the exterior. A leather interior allows your foot to breathe and absorbs moisture well. Good quality shoes should be lined inside completely.

[4] There should not be any visible glue anywhere on the shoe.

POLISH SHOES

Polishing your leather shoes is essential to maintaining the appearance and the quality of the leather. The market today is flooded with a vast array of shoe-cleaning products, from wipes to sprays and waxes to pastes. Below is a guide to the best care for your shoes.

Conditioning Your Shoes

Before you ever wear a new pair of leather shoes, treat them with a leather conditioner to soften the leather and prevent cracking, as wax can dry the leather over time.

How Often To Clean

Your shoes should be cleaned whenever necessary, and should be polished and treated monthly. Rub with a soft cloth between polishings, or else use one of the shoe-wipe products now on the market.

How To Clean

[1] Remove any laces from your shoes.

[2] Remove all dirt from the shoes with a soft cloth and leather cleaner, saddle soap, or simply a damp cloth. Towel- or air-dry.

[3] Remove salt stains with a white vinegar solution. One tablespoon of white vinegar mixed with a cup of hot water and rubbed onto the shoe with a cloth will remove the stain. Leave to air-dry before proceeding.

[4] Remove mildew from shoes with equal measures of rubbing alcohol and water applied with a sponge and left to air-dry.

[5] Use a wax or a cream polish. (A wax will stay on the surface whereas the leather will absorb the cream.) It is vital to color-match the product carefully. If you wish to cover up scratched leather, you will need to apply a colored wax or cream that is a shade lighter than the leather.

[6] Use polish sparingly: apply with a soft brush in a circular motion. Leave to air-dry for at least quarter of an hour.

[7] Shoe polish can be toxic: always wear gloves and dispose of finished containers carefully. Alternatives to beeswax polishes are vegetable or olive oils, applied with a cloth, and followed up by a buffing with petroleum jelly once dried. But test a small, inconspicuous area first.

[8] Once your product has dried, buff the leather to a shine, first with a shoe-cleaning brush, then with a soft cloth.

[9] Deal with offensive shoe odor by using baking soda. Sprinkle the inside of the shoe with baking soda and leave overnight. Shake out before wearing. Store your shoes with cedar blocks inside as an alternative.

SEW A BUTTON

Replacing buttons as you lose them from your dress shirts is a simple but essential skill.

Sewing A Two-hole Button

[1] Match the color of the thread to the color used for all the other buttons on the shirt.

[2] Try to find the button that fell off. If you can't, check the inside seams of the garment: many manufacturers sew in spare buttons there, just in case. Otherwise, you will need to find a suitable replacement, either from a clothing store, or by removing a less obvious button from elsewhere on the garment (for example, the cuff or the pocket).

[3] Run about six inches of thread through your needle and double the thread up so that both ends meet once threaded.

[4] Tie both ends together in a large knot.

[5] You will need to line the two holes up in the same direction as the button-hole, either vertically or horizontally.

[6] Push the needle through the back of the fabric at the place where the button needs to be and pull the thread through until the knot prevents you from pulling it any further.

[7] Thread the needle through one hole of the button on the front of the fabric.

[8] Push the button down the thread until it sits in the correct position.

[9] Thread the needle through the other buttonhole and pull it through to the back of the fabric.

[10] Insert a toothpick, needle, or pin through the stitch you have just made. This is to ensure that the thread doesn't attach the button too tightly against the fabric.

[11] Continue to push the needle from back to front, front to back, through the two holes until you feel it is secure.

[12] Remove the toothpick.

[13] With the needle pushed through to the front of the fabric, but not through a buttonhole, wrap the loose thread several times around the shank (the thread between the button and the front of the fabric).

[14] Push the needle through to the back, cut the thread, and tie the two ends securely.

Sewing A Four-hole Button

The button is sewed in exactly the same method, except that you should sew first two holes diagonally, then the other two, so that the stitching forms an "x" shape, unless the other buttons on the garment have been sewn in using two parallel lines.

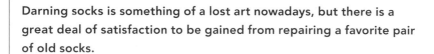

Darning socks is something of a lost art nowadays, but there is a great deal of satisfaction to be gained from repairing a favorite pair of old socks.

[1] Select your thread carefully. You need to match not only the color but also the type of thread to your sock. Sewing cotton will not do: embroidery thread or woolen thread will be more effective.

[2] Use a darning or embroidery needle with a larger eye. These needles are also blunter, which makes the process easier.

[3] Insert a light bulb into the sock, with the rounded end against the inside of the sock. You can buy specifically designed objects for this purpose, known as darning eggs. Alternatively, any smooth rounded object that will enable you to pass the needle over while slightly stretching the area to be repaired will do the job.

[4] Carefully trim any loose ends of thread from the hole.

[5] Do not knot the end of the thread.

[6] Use a running stitch from about a quarter-of-an-inch outside the hole, to make a series of vertical lines of thread. A running stitch is created by passing the needle from front to back and so on in equal distances.

[7] Be careful not to pull the thread too tightly, as it will pucker the material.

[8] Vertical lines need to be very closely positioned next to each other, at regular intervals. The woven repair must be tight to be effective.

[9] Once you have covered the entire hole with vertical lines of thread, to a quarter-of-an-inch away from the hole, turn the sock and begin to make horizontal stitches across the hole. This time you need to ensure that you weave the needle in and out of the threads you have already stitched.

The larger the hole the more difficult it will be to darn effectively. It is advisable to check regularly for signs of thinning fabric: if you can begin to see your flesh through the sock, it is time to carry out the repair. It will be far easier to weave your running stitches through the existing fabric than it will be to repair a bare hole.

This method can also be used to repair other woolens, such as gloves and sweaters.

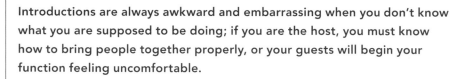

Introductions are always awkward and embarrassing when you don't know what you are supposed to be doing; if you are the host, you must know how to bring people together properly, or your guests will begin your function feeling uncomfortable.

[1] Use both first and last names and titles such as Doctor, Professor, Aunt, Uncle, etc., where appropriate.

[2] Introduce the person of lower status to the person of higher status, and the younger person to the older. Say the name of the most important person first. For example, "Ms. CEO, I'd like you to meet Mr. Sales Rep."

[3] If there is a considerable age difference, it is customary to defer to age, regardless of the social status of the two individuals.

[4] When introducing business colleagues to a client, the client should always be granted the higher status.

[5] Always introduce a man to a woman (although in business this rule does not apply).

[6] Don't say "introduce." Say "I'd like to present" or "I'd like you to meet." Avoid phrases such as "shake hands with" or "make you acquainted with."

[7] If the person you are introducing has a particular relationship to you (spouse, boss, aunt, interior designer, therapist), make it known, as it helps the other person to link them mentally to you, and may even give them something to talk about. Don't say "this is my friend," as it will make the other person feel like an outsider.

[8] Introduce an individual to a group and then the group to the individual. For example, "Dr. James Green, I'd like you to meet my colleagues, Michael Carter, Jane Roberts, and John Masters. Everyone, this is Dr. James Green."

[9] If you have forgotten someone's name, it is far better to apologize and admit that your memory has let you down, rather than avoid making an introduction, leaving your guests to sort it out amongst themselves.

[10] You may think it is a great idea to point out something that you feel two people have in common, but that won't necessarily make their initial conversation any easier. They may feel obliged to talk about this alleged common link, only to find that this supposed rich seam of conversation is exhausted almost immediately. Once you have introduced them, leave them to converse naturally, rather than have to follow your agenda.

Years ago a handshake was used to show another person that you were unarmed and friendly. Nowadays, the handshake is more social than life saving, but it is still one of the most important pieces of non-verbal communication you will ever use.

The Approach

Make eye contact and approach the other person with your right arm extended, at a slight downward angle with the palm vertical. Make sure you get close enough to them, or you'll overextend and may even have to bend forward, making you feel weak and awkward.

Making Contact

When you make contact with the other person's hand, don't just grip the fingers. Make sure that your palms meet and that the space between your thumb and first finger makes contact with theirs (it's also a great way to disable a potential bone-crusher).

Shake up and down once, while saying a word of greeting such as "Pleased to meet you." Maintain eye contact throughout. Avoid pumping your hand up and down repeatedly, and shake from the elbow, not from the shoulder.

Firm Or Limp?

No one likes a bone-crushing grip—it's aggressive and leaves the other person feeling, at worst pain, and at best that you've got something to prove. A handshake should be firm and should match the pressure exerted by the other person. Be aware that in some cultures (such as China and Japan) a handshake is noticeably softer than in the West, and in others still it isn't appropriate at all (for example, in Thailand, a slight bow called a *wai* is the customary form of greeting).

Power Games

Politicians are expert handshakers and use them to play power games. Watch two of them shaking hands and see which one manages to get his hand on top of the other's—that's a sign of dominance.

One Hand Only

A sincere handshake uses one hand only. Do not be tempted to involve your other hand either in the dreaded "double-grip," or to touch the person's arm or shoulder. A two-hander is supposed to convey warmth and sincerity, but can be very difficult to pull off convincingly. Only attempt the two-hander if you are very comfortable with it and it is sincerely meant, otherwise you will make the other person feel icky.

Stay Dry

If you suffer from sweaty palms, discreetly wipe your hands on your pants before a handshake. No one likes a clammy palm. If it's a big problem, a little antiperspirant on your palm wouldn't go amiss.

Believe it or not, there's a wrong way to get out of a chair. It's true that there are easier ways to injure yourself than using a less-than-efficient chair-exiting strategy. However, here is a more ergonomic method that uses less energy, places less stress on your back and neck, and feels easier too.

The Wrong Way

When you are sitting down, if your backside is at the back of the chair your center of gravity is far back as well. In order to get off the chair you must bring your center of gravity forward. Most people do this by putting their head back and leading with their chest, and if this isn't enough, they even jerk to gain momentum, throwing them forward but off-balance.

The Right Way

The most controlled and energy-efficient method starts with your head. You want to move forward and up while keeping your head in line with your neck and spine. Your alignment should not be rigidly straight, kinked by a pulled-back head, or overstretched by a chin dropped onto the chest.

[1] Place your feet flat on the ground with your knees facing forward.

[2] Think of a line going from the middle of your pelvis, through your neck, out of the top of your head, and rising into the sky.

[3] Now imagine that someone is gently pulling on this line to help you to move forward and up. Lead with the top of your head, bend at the waist, and bring your upper body forward and up as you think of sending your knees forward and away.

[4] Use your hands to push you upward. Press them gently on the seat of the chair next to your thighs, keeping your shoulders relaxed and your arms slightly bent.

[5] Keep your neck free as your head continues to rise forward and up, your back lengthens and widens, and your knees move forward and away.

[6] Rise in a single smooth and fluid movement. If you have to jerk to give yourself momentum, you are doing it wrong.

[7] Breath holding is very common during the simplest of activities. To prevent this, breathe in before you start moving, then breathe out as you rise. Take another breath after you are standing up.

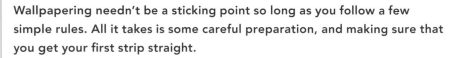

HANG WALLPAPER

Wallpapering needn't be a sticking point so long as you follow a few simple rules. All it takes is some careful preparation, and making sure that you get your first strip straight.

How Many Rolls?

First, decide how many rolls of wallpaper you need for the job. Measure the length of each wall, then multiply by the height of the room to give you a total surface area. Now, add ten percent to account for mistakes and compare it to the square-foot area per roll of wallpaper (this is written on the packet). Don't subtract space for doors and windows.

Preparation

The most important part of any interior-decoration job is surface preparation. Strip off old wallpaper, fill holes and cracks, sand the walls to remove any bumps, and then wipe with a clean damp cloth. Make sure you get rid of all irregularities, as these will show through the paper.

Cut strips of paper two inches longer than you need. Turn off the electricity and remove switch plates and plugs.

Roll Up

It is vital that your first strip be straight. Use a spirit level to draw a vertical line just over a roll's-width away from one corner. Begin papering near a window and work away from the window.

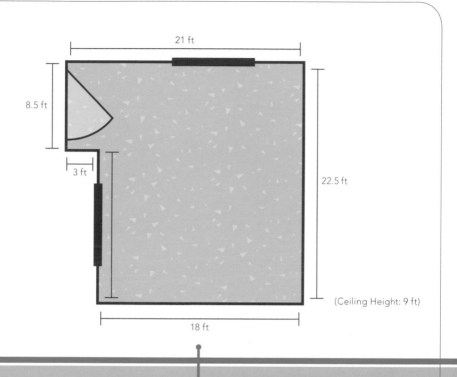

21 + 22.5 + 18 + 3 + 8.5 = 73

73 x 9 = 657

657 + 10% = 722.7 (Total Square Feet)

Apply The Paste

Make certain you have the right adhesive paste for the paper. Lightweight papers and heavy vinyl require special paste.

Lay a strip of wallpaper over a long table and apply paste to the whole strip, making sure you cover corners and edges thoroughly. You will need to concertina the paper over onto itself (pasted sides touching) so that you can apply paste to the whole strip, and then carry it to the wall. This is called "booking." Leave the paste to soak into the strip for a few minutes (check instructions on the paper).

Onto The Wall

Unhook the top part of the strip and stick it to the top of the wall, allowing an inch of overlap at the ceiling. Position the paper so that the edge lines up with your vertical line. Gently press the strip against the wall using a clean brush, then unhook the bottom half and smooth it into place. Now, smooth the whole strip, working from the top diagonal downward, to remove any air bubbles. Remove excess paste with a damp cloth.

Keeping Trim

Slowly trim the edges along the top and bottom using a sharp knife. Replace the blade if the paper begins to tear.

Second Strip

Apply the second strip using the same method, and butt the edges tightly against each other (do not overlap the edges).

Door, Windows, And Outlets

Hang the paper over the door or window and smooth it down, then make diagonal cuts in the paper at the corners, to allow you to smooth the paper into position. Trim to remove excess paper. Paper over an electrical outlet, then cut an "X" over the socket, and remove the flaps with a knife.

Painting is the quickest (and often the cheapest) way of freshening up a room or giving it a complete makeover.

Choosing Your Materials

It is essential that you use quality brushes and choose the right paint. Use brushes with natural bristles or a natural lamb's-wool roller for oil-based paint, and a synthetic brush or roller for emulsion (natural bristles go limp in water-based paint).

Use matt emulsion for walls and ceilings, vinyl silk for areas of high humidity, such as bathrooms and kitchens (or for children's bedrooms for ease of wiping clean), and gloss on woodwork. Oil-based paint is stain-resistant and is often used in bathrooms and kitchens. Measure the area of walls and ceilings and check coverage on the paint can so that you don't buy too much. Good quality paint goes onto the wall more smoothly, and gives greater coverage and a superior finish.

Prepare The Surfaces

Remove all furniture and drapes from the room. Remove dust and cobwebs with a vacuum cleaner and wet cloth, then fill any holes with filler and sand the walls smooth. You should spend as long preparing the surfaces as you do painting. If you strip anything back to the wood or plaster, apply a primer or the paint won't stick to the wood. Then, give the walls a once over with a low-phosphate household cleaner or commercial wall-cleaning product to remove stains such as grease or smoke that will soak through the new paint. Cover the floor with a thick canvas or drop-cloth (avoid using bedsheets as they are too thin and spilled paint will soak through).

Apply The Paint

Make sure there is adequate ventilation, and take regular breaks to avoid inhaling too many paint fumes.

Paint the ceiling first, then the walls, and finally the woodwork. Paint a three-inch strip along the edge of the ceiling where it meets the walls. This is called "cutting-in." You can paint the rest of the ceiling using a long-handled roller. Apply a second coat if required only when the first coat is dry.

Next the walls: Cut in along the top of the wall then start at the top corner of a wall and work downward and into the middle. Paint square sections going up and down, then across for an even finish. When using a roller avoid stopping in mid-stroke as this will leave a mark.

Cleaning Up

If you spill paint, wipe it up immediately as it will be harder to remove when it is dry (especially from fabrics).

Laying carpet needn't be a pile of trouble when you've got the right tools and a little know-how. And it can also save you a few pennies too, since carpet companies sometimes add a hefty fee for fitting. Why not fit it yourself and use the money you save to buy higher-quality carpet?

Prepare The Floor

If you have a wooden floor, remove all nails and surface irregularities—either hammer them in or pull them out. Secure loose floorboards. For masonry flooring, make sure it is clean and smooth.

Tackless Strip

The first job is to lay the tackless strip. This is a strip of wood with lots of tacks sticking out of it, which grips the carpet and holds it in place. Nail the strips around the edges of the room about a quarter-of-an-inch away from the wall and with the tacks pointing toward the wall. Don't lay the strip along doorways.

Carpet Padding

Install the underlay (carpet padding) with the waffle side upward, so that it butts up to the edge of the tackless strip (not over it). Do not overlap the edges of the underlay—butt them against each other. Use a staple-gun to staple the underlay every six inches (use glue with a masonry floor). Cover seams with duct tape.

Cutting The Carpet

Cut the carpet to size, allowing about six inches excess (which you will trim off later). Cut pile carpet along the back with a utility knife and cut loop-pile carpet from the front. If you need to use two or more pieces of carpet, lay the edge of the first piece over the second (with the pile facing in the same direction) and use it as a guide to cut a perfect straight edge. Place seaming tape under the edges, with the adhesive side facing up, and butt them together. Heat the tape with a seaming iron and press the edges firmly (a rolling pin is very effective here).

Laying The Carpet

Pile should face towards the door. Lay the carpet down along one wall and use a knee-kicker to attach it to the tackless strip, starting at one corner and working along the wall. Trim the excess carpet using a wall trimmer, holding it at an angle with its base on the floor. Use a stair tool to push the edges underneath the skirting board.

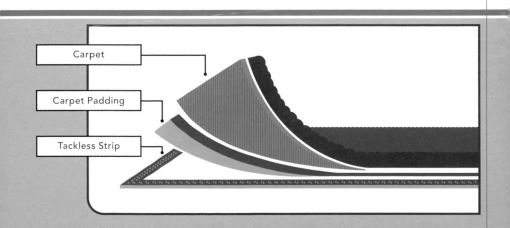

Carpet

Carpet Padding

Tackless Strip

Buying a sofa is a more involved decision than you might think.

The Size Of Your Sofa

Take the entrance to your house or apartment into careful consideration, as well as the size of your lounge room. Measure doorways; take a close look at the entrance or stairwell in your apartment block to make sure you can get the sofa into the house.

The Construction Of Your Sofa

Ask the sales personnel about how the sofa is made. Remember that the major signs of quality construction are all internal and hidden. Where possible, avoid sofas whose internal frames have been stapled together. Look for hardwood frames with glued and nailed joints as a sign of quality. Less expensive sofas have a pine construction.

Think about the quality of the cushions. Are they cheap foam or more luxurious down? What about the springs under the seats? Are you satisfied that they are of good quality? Test them out: sit down with some force and feel how the sofa responds. Ask the sales personnel to tell you the number of coils the springs have. The higher the number of coils, the better the quality.

Finally, test the arm rests to see how solid they feel. Is there any give in them?

The Look And Feel Of Your Sofa

Decide which basic design elements appeal to you most. Do you prefer a chic, contemporary single cushion, or the more traditional two or three? Do you like to be able to see the feet, or have them covered by fabric or fringing? What about the upholstery? Heavy-duty fabrics, soft chenilles, or cool leather?

If your household contains pets and children, this may influence your choice of fabric. Tweeds and patterned fabrics will show spills less than plain chenille. Feel the fabrics, too. Some will feel rough and less pleasant against bare skin.

The Comfort Factor

Sit on lots of sofas before you commit to buying one. Figure out what makes you most comfortable. Think about the people in your household and how they will sit on it. Are they loungers and recliners, or straight-backed types who like lots of lower back support? Can you rest your feet on the floor easily? What does it feel like with two (or more) people sitting on it?

FRAME A PICTURE

A well-constructed homemade picture frame is of enormous satisfaction and can be tailor-made to complement the artwork you have in mind.

You Will Need

The wood of your choice (e.g., hard maple), measured to allow a few inches of space on either side of the piece of art to be framed. Also needed is:

Glass cut to the same size
Wood glue
Panel nails
Picture frame wire
Two small screws
Cardboard measured to size
Plywood measured to size
Router
Sander
Power saw

Basic Method

[1] Using a power saw, cut the wood into four carefully measured pieces, with a forty-five-degree angle at each end to make the frame.

[2] Use the router to gradually carve out a groove that will hold the artwork, glass, and back covers in place.

[3] Sand the wood and add a finish of your choice: wax, varnish, or paint.

[4] Glue the wood together with wood glue and clamp it in place to dry overnight.

[5] If you wish to mount your artwork, select a suitable material and cut it to size. Take time to select material that will complement the picture in terms of color and texture.

[6] Carefully place the glass, the mount, and the artwork inside the frame.

[7] Insert the cardboard and the sheet of plywood for the outer back panel. If the artwork is still moving freely inside the frame, add further layers of filler until it is secured.

[8] Fix the plywood to the back of the frame with small panel nails.

[9] Finally, attach the picture-frame wire to two small screws fixed into the back panel, making sure the screws are centrally positioned.

Getting Creative

The basic frame can be decorated in a variety of methods, according to your taste and to the picture you wish to display. Mosaic tiles, mirror strips, stencils, and varnished *decoupage* are all simple and attractive ways to draw further attention to the frame. Where the frame is intended for a mirror, a more elaborate finish would work well. However, if you wish it to frame treasured artwork, you may wish to keep it simple so as not to detract from the piece itself. In this case a simple routed groove can add a simple yet attractive finish to the frame.

Wear protective eye-goggles when using power tools. If in doubt, have the pieces of wood pre-cut for you by the supplier.

Shelving is an effective open-storage solution that doesn't sacrifice floor space, especially in kids' rooms.

Alcove Or Closet Shelving

The easiest way to erect shelves is to place them in an alcove or closet. Make sure the shelves are the correct depth for the space and do not stick out beyond the front of the alcove. Cut three wooden support blocks for each shelf—a long one for the back wall and two shorter ones for the sides. Use a spirit level to make them horizontal. Hide the side blocks by attaching a lip to the front of the shelf, or else cut the front-block edge at a forty-five-degree angle (with the leading angle at the top). Screw the shelves into the blocks for maximum stability.

Shelves look best when they are equidistant. If you need taller shelves for bigger books and objects, put them at the bottom, with the smallest shelves at the top.

Bracket Shelving

Mark two vertical lines on the wall using a spirit level. Hold a bracket against the line and mark the holes through it. Drill holes in masonry using a masonry bit. For a stud partition wall, make holes in the stud using a wooden drill bit (tap the wall to locate them—they are usually sixteen inches apart). Attach one bracket to the wall, then place the second bracket on the other vertical guideline and rest the spirit level on both brackets. When the brackets are level, mark the holes on the wall through the second bracket, drill holes, and attach brackets to the wall.

Shelving System

These allow greater flexibility and are easy to erect. All you have to do is attach the first support mount to the wall, using a spirit level to ensure it is vertical. Then line up the second support by attaching a shelf and brackets. Use a spirit level to make it horizontal, then mark the screw holes.

Bowed Shelves

Sagging shelves are taking too much weight for their thickness, or else they have inadequate support. Fix this by adding a back-wall support, if there isn't one already, or attach a wooden or metal lip to the front. With wooden shelves, a hardwood shelf will support more weight than a softwood shelf (relative to its thickness). Composites such as medium-density fiberboard (MDF) are also a good choice.

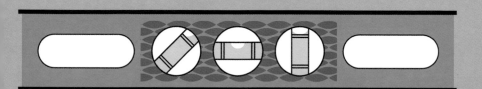

MAKE A BED WITH HOSPITAL CORNERS

Many of us use fitted sheets which fit snugly over the mattress, but if you still use flat sheets, then hospital corners will give you a crisp and smooth bed. You can't beat the feeling of sliding into a properly made bed, so here's how to make one.

Bottom Sheet

Lay the sheet over the mattress so that the middle crease runs down the middle of the mattress and leave enough room to tuck the sheet underneath on all four sides.

Tuck the top part of the sheet under the mattress at the foot and head. Starting at one corner, pull the sheet taut long ways with one hand under the mattress to keep it taut. Now use the other hand to grip the flap hanging down the long side of the bed about a foot away from the end. Keeping it taut, lay it on top of the bed so that it forms a right-angled triangle.

Tuck in the remaining sheet on the long side, then bring the triangle of material down again and rearrange it so that when you tuck it in you can make a straight edge at the corner. Repeat on the other three corners, making sure that you pull the sheet taut to maintain a crisp and wrinkle free surface. The surface tension also helps to keep the folded corners in place.

Top Sheet

Place the top sheet on top of the bed so that the crease runs down the middle. You may either tuck the bottom two corners as described above, or leave it looser, depending on how much foot room you prefer.

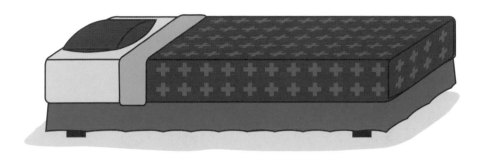

Blankets

Cover the sheet with a blanket or bedspread and tuck the foot end into the bottom of the mattress, leaving the long sides hanging down. Pull them at the toes to make a three-inch pleat to allow room for the feet to move. Pull the blanket and top sheet over the head end, then fold them back again and place the plumped up pillow on top. Leave the sides untucked, unless you like your bed to feel like a straightjacket.

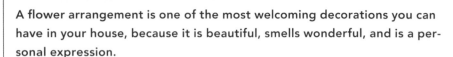

ARRANGE FLOWERS

A flower arrangement is one of the most welcoming decorations you can have in your house, because it is beautiful, smells wonderful, and is a personal expression.

[1] Choose flowers that are full of vitality, that stand up straight, and that look crisp, plump, firm, and vibrant. If the stems are limp or the flowers are dull, curling, or starting to turn, don't use them.

[2] In order to stay fresh, the flowers need to be in clean containers, free from bacteria, with an adequate supply of water. If you are using floral foam, soak it in a bowl for about twenty seconds and place it in a clean vase. Bottled water is preferable to tap water, as the minerals in the latter inhibit water uptake.

[3] The water temperature is important: warm water will encourage the buds to open, and cool water will make them last longer and bloom more slowly.

[4] Don't improvise. Before you begin, visualize how you want the finished arrangement to look. Be aware of where the arrangement will be displayed. What shape will it be—fan, pyramid, ball?

[5] Cut stems under running water at a forty-five-degree angle with sharp scissors. This allows maximum flow of water into the stems. Do not snap the stems with your fingers. Remove leaves that will be below the water line. Cover the base with foliage to hide the floral foam.

[6] Begin the arrangement by placing basic structural flowers that will create the overall shape. Do not add any more flowers until you are happy with this shape, as many poor arrangements can usually be traced back to mistakes early on. Place the longest stems in the center of your bouquet.

[7] Don't just think about balancing colors—focus also on shapes, sizes, and textures. "Line" flowers are tall and straight and are useful for creating outline shapes, height, and width. "Mass" flowers are generally round and usually provide the color and interest. Smaller and more delicate "filler" flowers soften and pull the whole arrangement together.

[8] The arrangement should be three-dimensional. Inexperienced flower arrangers make the common mistake of facing all their blooms on one plane, rather than turning them at subtly different angles.

[9] Large and dark flowers should go at the bottom, and lighter, smaller flowers at the top and edges.

[10] Combine buds and blooms with half-open flowers. Buds generally look better at the top of an arrangement, open flowers at the bottom center, and half-open ones in between. Each flower should have its own space and should not touch its neighbors.

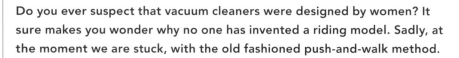
Do you ever suspect that vacuum cleaners were designed by women? It sure makes you wonder why no one has invented a riding model. Sadly, at the moment we are stuck, with the old fashioned push-and-walk method.

As the American Chiropractic Association advises—vacuum using a "fencer's stance." Put all your weight on one foot, then step forward and back with the other foot as you push the vacuum forward and back. Use the back foot as a pivot when you turn.

Always check for blockages. If the last person to use the cleaner was careless, chances are they've clogged it up with coins and tissues—something you would never do. There's no point lugging ten pounds of squealing machinery around the house sucking at twenty percent of its capacity. While you've got it in pieces, check the belt, which tends to stretch and wear out. It needs changing once every six months, even if it hasn't snapped or torn.

Run the vacuum with an extension cord—no more unplugging—now it will stretch all over the house. Flick the switch and start cleaning.

- Pass over areas with light soiling three times, but use five to seven passes for heavily soiled areas that are used frequently—the thoroughfares. Change direction occasionally to help raise the pile and reduce matting

- Dust piles up along the edge of carpeting, so use an attachment to access cracks and along the top of the skirting board

- Vacuum air-conditioning vents (including the one on your PC)

- Wipe a damp rag along the tops of doors and window frames

- Do not vacuum the stove or chimney. The soot will seep out of the machine and you'll spread it everywhere

- Don't vacuum thin lightweight rugs (e.g., terrycloth bathroom mats) that will just get chewed up. If you have to stand on one corner to stop it from disappearing, you should be beating it outside instead.

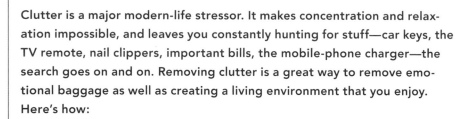

REMOVE CLUTTER

Clutter is a major modern-life stressor. It makes concentration and relaxation impossible, and leaves you constantly hunting for stuff—car keys, the TV remote, nail clippers, important bills, the mobile-phone charger—the search goes on and on. Removing clutter is a great way to remove emotional baggage as well as creating a living environment that you enjoy. Here's how:

[1] Little and often: Don't try to clear several months' of junk in one go. Your house has been cluttering up for months, years even. Develop a daily system to allow you to rein in your rat's nest gradually, otherwise it's the equivalent to crash dieting without changing your long-term eating habits—the weight piles back on, and then some.

[2] Set a timer and allow yourself a slot each day—between fifteen minutes to an hour. Don't pull out the entire contents of a wardrobe if you won't have time to sort it out, otherwise you will create more mess than you started with.

[3] From DVDs to scissors, shoes, pencils, and dishes, designate a correct place for every item in your house, and force yourself to return it when you have finished.

[4] Label three large boxes: GIVE AWAY, THROW AWAY, and PUT AWAY. When the first box is full, take it to the goodwill shop or thrift store. Don't dump the box in the garage.

[5] Start at the door and work clockwise around a room. This will stop you from getting distracted or overwhelmed. If you're interrupted or run out of time, you can start where you left off.

[6] Tackle all paper clutter as soon as it enters the house. As a rule, a piece of paper should pass through your hands only once. If it's a bill, pay it immediately. Keep a file for your paid bills, but shred them after six months. Shred junk mail immediately.

[7] With each item of clutter ask: "Do I love this?"; "Do I have another one the same, and if so, do I need two?"; "Have I used this recently?"; "Does it make me smile?"

[8] Get rid of anything that doesn't make you smile.

[9] Throw out clothes you haven't worn for a year. Don't keep clothes that you plan to slim into. Instead, lose the weight and treat yourself to some new threads. That's a much better incentive for shedding a few pounds!

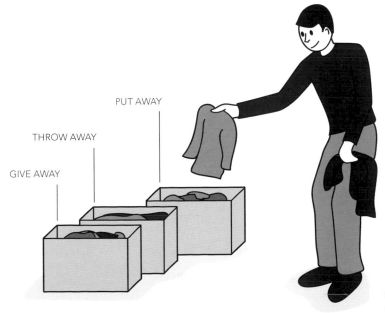

PUT AWAY

THROW AWAY

GIVE AWAY

TREAT STAINS

There are a few basic rules to bear in mind when treating most stains on fabric.

[1] Treat the stain as soon as possible.

[2] Pre-soak stained fabric in cold water before laundering, since many stains can be set by hot water.

[3] Place the stain face down on a paper towel, then apply stain remover to the back so that the stain doesn't soak through the fabric.

[4] Once you have pre-treated the stain, wash the fabric in the hottest water temperature the care label allows.

[5] Use a biological or enzyme-based detergent.

[6] Check for signs of the stain before drying, as the drying process can also set the stain and make it very difficult to remove.

Treating Stains On Fabrics For Dry-cleaning

If the fabric is not washable, you can apply dry-cleaning fluid to the garment with a sponge, then allow it to air-dry. (Never put garments treated with dry-cleaning fluid in the washing machine as it is a fire risk.)

If you are unsure, take it to be dry-cleaned and explain the nature of the stain.

Treating Specific Stains

Sometimes different stains are best treated in different ways.

Oil- or chocolate-based stains: olive oil, gravy, salad dressing, etc.

Use dishwashing detergent on the back of the stain.

Pre-treat before washing with color-safe bleach.

Milk-based stains: eggnog, milkshake, etc.

Apply a paste of detergent to the back of the stain.

Tannin-based stains: red wine, grape juice

Blot with cold water immediately then use salt to absorb the liquid.

Soak in cold water.

Before washing, apply color-safe bleach.

Tomato-based stains: ketchup, spaghetti sauce, etc.

Club soda applied to the back of the stain should break it up.

Pre-soak in cold water.

Wash at the highest temperature you can, pre-treated with color-safe bleach.

Chewing gum

Freeze the gum by applying ice packed in a plastic bag.

Once the gum is hard, chip off as much as you can with a blunt knife.

Soak the area with color-safe bleach before laundering.

Candle wax

Chip away as much of the wax as you can with a blunt knife.

Place the stain between several layers of paper towels or greaseproof paper.

Set an iron to a warm temperature and press gently.

Pre-treat the back of the stain with color-safe bleach before laundering.

Usually, the cause of a clogged sink is waste food that has built up in the U-bend of the trap. As a basic precaution, always avoid emptying poultry or other fat down the drain. It may be a free-running liquid when it's hot out of the oven, but as soon as it meets cold water, it solidifies. Even if you try flushing it out each time with hot water, over time enough build-up will remain to cause a clog.

If you suspect your sink has become clogged by grease, there are several special detergents on the market that will dissolve the grease for you.

However, if your sink is clogged by something altogether more stubborn, here is how to unclog it in ten easy steps.

[1] Try to release the blockage using a plunger. There are several variations on the traditional plunger on the market today, including power plungers which build up air then release it at some force so that the clog is often broken into smaller pieces and disperses easily.

[2] Cover the drain with the rubber end of a plunger and turn on the tap until the water just covers the plunger by about a half-inch.

[3] Block the overflow outlet with a rag so that you can build up more suction with the plunger.

[4] Repeatedly move the wooden handle of the plunger up and down.

[5] If plunging your sink doesn't fix the problem, and the clog does not respond to hand-snaking with a simple plumber's snake, you will need to remove the U-bend of the pipe.

[6] First, empty the space beneath the sink and have a bowl in place there to catch any water.

[7] You need to unscrew the trap by taking off two nuts. The first will be attached to the bowl and the second to the plastic waste pipe.

[8] Empty everything that is stuck in the trap.

[9] Fix the trap back again. First screw on the second nut you removed that joined the trap to the plastic waste pipe. Then fix the other nut to the bowl.

[10] Your sink should now run freely.

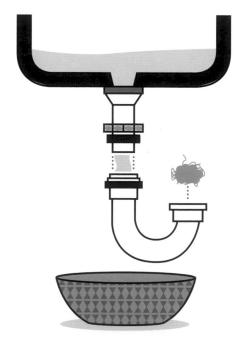

REPAIR A LEAKING FAUCET

There are as many makes of faucet on the market as there are break-fast cereals, so when you need replacement parts, take the old faucet with you to the hardware store so that you get the right model.

Turn off the water and open the faucet to run off any water in the pipes.

Cover the sink with a towel to protect the porcelain from falling tools and to stop small items, such as nuts and washers, from falling down the drain. Tape the jaws of wrenches to stop them from scratching the faucet.

The most common causes of a leaking faucet are old gaskets, or O-rings, and corroded valve seats. Sometimes, the leak can be repaired simply by tightening the packing nut at the base of the handle.

Stem Faucet

On some faucets you must remove the handle to unbolt the bonnet. Unscrew the top of the faucet and remove the handle to reveal the bonnet. Remove the bonnet with pliers or an adjustable wrench, then remove the valve system by turning it in the direction that would normally shut off the water. This is what the valve system looks like:

Undo the screw at the bottom of the valve assembly, then remove and replace either the washer or O-ring, or valve seat as necessary. Replace with a washer of identical diameter and thickness, and with the same size inner hole.

Reassemble the valve assembly and replace it in the tap. Screw the handle back on if necessary.

Single-lever Faucet

This is a harder repair job than a stem faucet and often requires specialist tools.

At the base of the handle, unscrew the setscrew with a hex wrench. Lift out the handle-and-ball assembly.

If the spout has been dripping, remove and replace the two rubber valve seats and steel springs using long-nose pliers.

Check the ball for corrosion. To reassemble, line up the peg on the side of the cavity with the oblong slot on the ball.

SHOVEL SNOW

For thousands of households, a heavy covering of snow every winter sends us reaching for the snow shovel. But what appears at first as an innocuous task should come with its own health warning. For the fit and active a half-hour spent shoveling snow counts as a daily dose of moderate activity. For the more sedentary, and those at risk from heart disease, it can be a very different story.

Take Precautions

If you think you may be at risk, check with your doctor before you begin. Warm your body before you begin to shovel: stretch out your muscles and take a warm shower. This will reduce your chances of straining a muscle. Avoid caffeine or nicotine prior to shoveling, as these are stimulants that will raise your heart rate before you even begin.

Dress Well

Be aware of the temperature outside. Dress in several layers in order to protect yourself from hypothermia, and to enable you to remove clothing a layer at a time as your body heats up from the exertion.

Choose Your Equipment Carefully

Ideally, you will need a smaller shovel, as this will ensure you cannot overload it and put too great a strain on your heart. A good shovel to use is one with a blade that will enable you to push some of the snow away rather than lift it. Check the length of the handle that suits you.

Begin Steadily

At first, lift only very small amounts of snow on your shovel. This eases your body into what can otherwise be a sudden burst of heavy lifting. You can even begin during the snowfall, so that you can shift snow while it is still soft and ensure that the task of clearing it totally is carried out in stages. Avoid throwing the shovelsful over your shoulder, too. Taking regular breaks every few minutes is important, even for the very fit: very cold temperatures mean that your body will have to work far harder.

Once The Snow Is Cleared

Check for ice beneath the snow and chisel that away. Then dust the pathway with rock salt or calcium chloride pellets to prevent it from icing over. Sand will also give you a firmer grip underfoot.

Know When To Stop

At the first signs of feeling too cold, take a break and warm up inside. Likewise, if you feel any pain or shortness of breath you need to stop.

For many, a perfect deep-green lawn is the stuff of fantasy. Achieving it is simple with a decent mower and a basic understanding of the principles of lawn maintenance.

[1] Ensure that the blades on your rotary mower are kept sharp. A dull blade can be replaced inexpensively and will give a much better finish to your lawn. Ideally, you will need to sharpen or replace your blades every spring, when it is also advisable to have your mower serviced.

[2] Always mow the lawn when it is completely dry; cutting wet grass can be a disaster and can spread organisms harmful to the grass. The only exception to this is if a long period of rainfall leaves the lawn too long. Even if not thoroughly dry, it is better to mow than not to.

[3] Pay close attention to the setting of the blades on your mower. You should never cut the grass back too far, as very short grass will only send out a very short root system, leaving it weak and vulnerable to drought. It will also enable weeds to establish themselves in the lawn. Aim to remove a third of the length of the grass and no more.

[4] Different varieties of grasses have different recommended growing heights. Determine the variety of your lawn and find out its recommended height. Then you will need to maintain the grass to within these recommendations, ensuring it doesn't grow more than a third higher than this.

[5] Where your grass has grown too high, it is crucial that you do not hack off too much in one mowing. Cut the grass by a minimum amount the first time, then come back forty-eight hours later and give it another mowing in a different direction.

[6] Continue to cut the grass into the fall for as long as it appears to still be growing. When growth tails off, cut the lawn down by another half-inch or so, as a shorter lawn through the winter will stay healthier.

[7] The decision whether or not to remove clippings is a matter of personal choice: as fertilizer it goes a long way to keeping your grass green, but the clippings can look unsightly as they dry out.

An essential job, if a much dreaded one. Here's how to do it.

[1] Vacuum or sweep the floor thoroughly.

[2] Remove any sticky substances with a blunt knife or a windshield ice scraper.

[3] Fill a bucket with warm water and whatever quantity of detergent is indicated on the packaging.

[4] Never use hot water.

[5] Check that the detergent you are using is suitable for the floor covering. Some modern laminate flooring or polyurethane-coated hardwood floors cannot tolerate harsh detergents. You can buy special products in the cleaning-product aisles of most supermarkets.

[6] Fill a second bucket with cold water.

[7] For smooth, untextured floors, a sponge-mop with a self-squeezing device is the best type of mop to use. If your floor is textured, a loose, cotton-fiber mop head will work best.

[8] If the floor is very dirty, marked, or greasy, you may need to begin by cleaning it the old-fashioned way. Using a dual-textured sponge or scrub brush, agitate the water and soak your cleaning implement in it. Then, on your hands and knees, scrub a small area of floor in sweeping circular motions, first clockwise, then counter-clockwise. This will lift the most stubborn stains.

[9] Now, immerse your mop in the water/detergent mix.

[10] Squeeze the excess water out against the side of the bucket. Do not use your bare hands, as mops can pick up sharp objects from the floor that can cut your skin.

[11] Begin to mop the floor in the far corner of the room, away from the door.

[12] Move methodically across the room in broad figure-of-eight motions, overlapping each stroke.

[13] Move backward across the room, parallel to the baseboard of one wall.

[14] From time to time, plunge the mop into the cold water to rinse, then into the detergent mix again.

[15] It will also help if you flip the mop over frequently so that debris from the mop isn't left on the newly cleaned areas of the floor.

[16] As you work, try to keep your back straight.

[17] Use your arms to make the figure-of-eight, and avoid twisting your upper body with your spine.

[18] Squeeze out the excess as before.

[19] Change the water in both buckets as it gets dirty.

[20] Leave the floor to air-dry before walking on it.

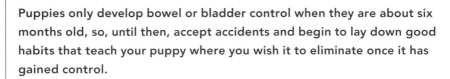

Puppies only develop bowel or bladder control when they are about six months old, so, until then, accept accidents and begin to lay down good habits that teach your puppy where you wish it to eliminate once it has gained control.

[1] Spend as much time as you are able to with your puppy in these early days. Take the puppy outdoors every forty-five minutes in good weather, so that it can begin to develop the habit of toileting outdoors.

[2] As the dog gets older, the length of time between trips outdoors can be greater. Establish a routine so that the dog gets to know when it will be taken out.

[3] Watch your puppy carefully so that you become familiar with the telltale behavior that precedes its need to go.

[4] If you see this behavior when the puppy is indoors, scoop it up and take it outside immediately.

[5] As you catch your puppy in the act of eliminating outdoors, give a clear command as it's doing so. Trainers often recommend "Hurry!" as an appropriate command. Over time this will trigger the dog's movements and encourage toileting on command.

[6] Always praise your puppy after it toilets outdoors, both verbally and with food treats.

[7] If you need to leave the puppy alone before it is house-trained, cover the floor in the room where it stays with newspaper. Gradually reduce the papered area as it begins to confine itself to one toileting area.

[8] At night, the puppy will be unwilling to toilet in its own sleeping area. Put it in a bed or a crate in your bedroom, or else within earshot so that you can hear whenever it begins to get restless. This is your cue to take it outdoors to toilet.

[9] Do not use the crate as a punishment. Make it comfortable and appealing, with bedding, water, and a few toys. Only confine it to its crate for short periods of time, and never longer than two hours.

[10] Never punish a puppy for an accident. This will only confuse it, and may set its house-training back. Ignore accidents and praise all successes.

[11] However, if you see the puppy is about to eliminate indoors, a firm "No!" and a swift exit will reinforce the appropriate behavior.

GOOD BOY!

HOUSE-TRAIN YOUR CAT

Cats can be routinely house-trained far more quickly than dogs. A few days should be all that is required to teach your kitten to use a litter box if you follow a few basic rules.

[1] Fill a litter box with a couple of inches of odorless litter.

[2] Make sure the litter box is in an easily accessible place.

[3] For the first day or two, keep the kitten, its box, and its food and water in a small quiet room.

[4] As soon as the kitten wakes in the morning, carry it gently to the litter box.

[5] Clean the box out on a daily basis and wash it out thoroughly with hot water every week.

[6] When the kitten is successfully using the litter box, you can let it explore the rest of the house. If necessary, place an additional box elsewhere in the house, particularly if the house is large, or if you have any other cats.

[7] If you need to relocate the box, do so gradually, an inch or two per day so as not to confuse the kitten.

How To Deal With Accidents

If the kitten misses the litter box or messes somewhere else in the house, it is vital that you do not scold for this behavior. Here's what to do instead:

[1] Clean up the mess thoroughly so that any trace of scent is removed from the area. This will discourage the kitten from using the area again.

[2] Check to see that the box doesn't intimidate your kitten. If it has messed in a corner or under furniture, it is a clear sign that the location of the box makes it feel vulnerable. Buy or make a cover, or move the box so that it is not placed in a corner and can be easily escaped from if necessary.

[3] If you have used any soap-based products to clean the box, the scent may have discouraged the kitten from using it. Leave some soiled litter in the box to prompt it.

[4] Confine the kitten and its tray to one room again for a day or so. This should encourage it to return to the litter box.

[5] It is advisable to have a vet check your kitten over in case its inability to be litter-trained is caused by any medical disorder, such as a urinary tract infection.

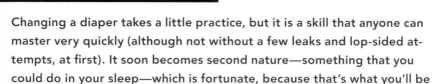
CHANGE A DIAPER

Changing a diaper takes a little practice, but it is a skill that anyone can master very quickly (although not without a few leaks and lop-sided attempts, at first). It soon becomes second nature—something that you could do in your sleep—which is fortunate, because that's what you'll be doing! Meanwhile, here's a step-by-step guide to start you off.

[1] Wash and dry your hands.

[2] If you are using a vinyl-padded changing-mat, it's a good idea to place a terrycloth towel on it to soak up any leaks if the baby passes water during the changing. Also, a bare changing-mat feels cold, even in a warm room.

[3] Lay the baby down on her back and unfasten the diaper tabs.

[4] Hold her ankles together with one hand and lift her bottom gently into the air, then fold the front of the soiled diaper over, unsoiled side up, so that the contents are covered.

[5] Wipe away poop from the genitals with baby-wipes or wet cotton wool. With a girl, always wipe from front to back, away from her vagina. This reduces the chance of getting feces and bacteria into it. Be vigilant when using baby-wipes, as overuse can dry and irritate the baby's skin.

[6] Clean the bottom. Then towel dry the whole area. Apply a barrier cream to any sore spots.

[7] Remove the soiled diaper and replace with a clean one. The top half of the clean diaper—the one with the tabs—should go underneath the baby's bottom. Bring the bottom half up between the baby's legs, which should be spread quite widely to prevent the diaper from bunching uncomfortably and chafing.

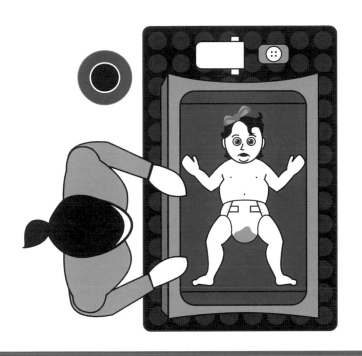

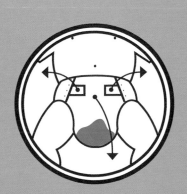
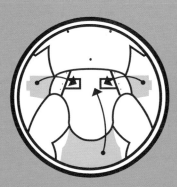

[8] Bring the front of the diaper up to the baby's waist, below the umbilical cord for newborns (it needs to stay dry). Fasten the tapes on both sides so that the diaper fits snugly, without pinching the skin or being too tight. You should be able to slip two fingers into the waistband of a comfortable diaper, but it shouldn't be so loose that it flaps around.

[9] Tip any poop from inside the soiled diaper into the toilet. Re-tape the soiled diaper around its contents, place it in a plastic bag, and put it in the trash.

[10] Dress your baby and wash your hands thoroughly.

Diaper Rash

All babies get diaper rash, some more frequently than others. It is especially common when a baby has diarrhea or is teething. The best treatment is to change the diaper more regularly and give the bottom some fresh air (let the baby play without a diaper for fifteen minutes—hard on your nerves, but good for the diaper rash). Speak to your doctor or health consultant if you are concerned.

HOLD A BABY

If you have never held a baby before, it can be intimidating. Be assured, they won't break and, if you follow the tips below, they'll feel comfortable, safe, and happy with you.

Cradling A Baby

[1] Stand close to the person who is handing you the baby and lean your body in toward theirs.

[2] Use both hands.

[3] The hand facing the baby's head needs to cradle the head and neck gently, as a baby cannot support his or her head properly for the first few months of life.

[4] Use the other arm to support the bottom.

[5] Gently turn the baby so that the head is now pointing in the opposite direction and rest the head and neck on the opposite arm.

[6] The baby's head should nestle in the crook of your elbow comfortably, so that your free arm can now run under the length of the baby.

Holding A Baby Against Your Shoulder

[1] Alternatively, from step 4, you can turn the baby into a vertical position, all the time ensuring you keep the head and neck safe.

[2] Rest the baby against your shoulder.

[3] If the baby is against your left shoulder, use your left arm to support its bottom, and the right to support its head.

[4] Don't remove your right hand: the baby's head will loll backward.

Burping A Baby

[1] From step 4 above, turn the baby as before.

[2] Gently turn the baby over so that it is lying face down.

[3] Your forearm should be supporting its body and the baby's head can be nestled in against the crook of your elbow.

[4] Your hand should support the baby between the legs.

[5] With your free hand, steady the baby and gently rub its back.

Always talk gently to a baby and smile into the child's face. What you say doesn't matter as much as the way you say it. A soft and gentle tone and repetitive words are soothing and reassuring for a baby.

Carrying A Baby In A Sling

This is a great way to keep a baby close to you whenever you need to have two free hands. It may help if you practice with another adult until you have perfected the art.

All baby slings come with clear instructions. If in doubt, ask the sales personnel for assistance when you buy your sling.

DECORATE A CHRISTMAS TREE

If you have ever wondered why store-display Christmas trees always look better than your best domestic attempts, you may benefit from some insider tips from the professionals.

[1] Spend time to ensure that your tree is standing vertical and is symmetrical. A leaning tree will never look appealing, even with the best decorations. Stand the tree away from radiators and other heat sources, and away from doorways.

[2] Always place the lights on first, followed by the garlands, and finally the decorations.

[3] If your tree is placed in a corner, there is no point in decorating areas that won't be seen.

[4] Check that the lights are working. Place them around every major branch on the inside of the tree and on the middle of the branches, not at the tips. If you start at the base and work up, there's less chance that you'll run out of lights with a large chunk of tree left over.

[5] You should use about one hundred lights for every vertical foot of tree. Don't be afraid to mix and match colors, but remember that simplicity usually gives the best results—tiny, static white lights are classier than a Vegas light show. Faceted lights give maximum sparkle. Glowing and twinkling lights are more sophisticated than chasers and flashers.

[6] Lay the garland loosely, so that it hangs down in an arc between branches, rather than being pulled tight. Start at the top and work down and around the tree. Use garland sparingly at the top of the tree and increase the amount as you work downward, otherwise the tree will look top-heavy.

[7] Use several larger identical feature ornaments combined with smaller filler ornaments. Space out the larger feature ornaments first, about ten every two vertical feet of tree. Then, fill in the gaps with smaller ones. Repeating patterns or clusters of three filler baubles is very effective.

[8] When buying ornaments, stick to two or three complementary colors. Ornaments should be placed inside the tree as well as hung from the tips of branches, to give the tree a much fuller effect.

[9] Avoid hanging baubles from the bottom of the tree. They should end at the bottom of the foliage.

[10] Invest in an impressive feature decoration (star, angel, etc.) to adorn the top of the tree.

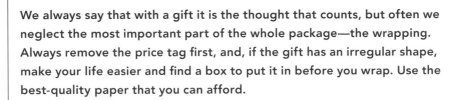

We always say that with a gift it is the thought that counts, but often we neglect the most important part of the whole package—the wrapping. Always remove the price tag first, and, if the gift has an irregular shape, make your life easier and find a box to put it in before you wrap. Use the best-quality paper that you can afford.

[1] Place the box on the wrapping paper and unroll enough paper to cover it, allowing for an extra two inches of overlap. Make sure there is enough paper to cover the ends completely when folded down (this depends on the thickness of the box). Getting the amount of extra paper right is key to tidy wrapping. If you have to fold over too much surplus, your edges will be bulky. This is especially true of the end flaps.

[2] Place the object in the center of the gift-wrap and bring one end over to the center of the top. Secure it with a small piece of clear masking tape (so it can be removed from the gift without spoiling it).

[3] Fold the opposite edge over one inch (this makes a tidy edge and gives the illusion of thicker paper) and bring it to the top of the middle; pull tight and tape down.

[4] Turn the box so that one of the open ends is facing you. Press the vertical sides inwards and smooth against the edge of the box to form two triangular flaps at the top and bottom of the edge. Crease the edges of the flaps to define the edges of the box.

[5] Bring down the upper flap and tape; repeat with the bottom flap.

[6] Turn the box so that it rests on its closed end and repeat steps 4 and 5 with the other open end.

[7] Turn the box over so the seamless side is on the bottom. Then wrap a length of ribbon lengthwise around the box, cross it over on the seam edge, and bring it around the box width-wise. Tie a double-knot where the ribbon meets on top of the box and cut the ribbon, leaving six inches to spare.

[8] Make the two ends of ribbon curl by running it along the edge of a pair of scissors and your thumb.

[9] Attach a gift tag by sliding it under the ribbon and secure it with a small piece of tape.

There are hundreds of knots and each is suited to a different task: joining ropes, securing objects, shortening ropes, etc. Some need tension to keep them together; others rely on their own internal tension. Here are ten useful knots to get you started.

Overhand Knot

The simplest of all knots, it is used as the basis for many others, and is used as a stopping knot.

Figure-Eight Knot

A basic rock climbing knot, and useful for "tying in" (attaching ropes to your climbing harness).

Cat's Paw

Used for attaching a rope to a hook. It doesn't slip and doesn't need rope tension to stay secure. Make two loops and twist them inward for two complete turns, then feed the hook through the end loops.

Fisherman's Knot

Used for joining two thin lines (e.g., fishing line), it consists of two interlocking overhand knots, pulled tight against each other.

Sheepshank

Use this knot to shorten rope that is fastened at both ends.

Half Hitch

A temporary attaching knot.

Sailor's Knot

Two half hitches, useful for making lines taut (washing line, tent line).

Sheet Bend

A better way of joining two ends than the reef knot.

The Reef Knot (aka Square Knot)

Probably one of the most popular and best known knots. Often used for tying two ends of rope together.

Fisherman's Bend (aka Anchor Bend)

A simple way of attaching a rope to a ring or anchor. Can be united easily without becoming jammed up under strain. Secure the free end to stop it coming loose.

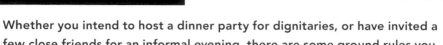

Whether you intend to host a dinner party for dignitaries, or have invited a few close friends for an informal evening, there are some ground rules you should follow when setting the table.

[1] Cover the table with a white linen tablecloth, ensuring that the middle crease runs down the center of the table in a straight line. The ends of the tablecloth should overhang the table by about eighteen inches for a seated meal. (For a buffet it should reach the floor.)

[2] Fold napkins elegantly and position them in the center of each diner's place (they may also go on the bread-and-butter plate or to the left of the forks).

[3] Cutlery is always positioned an inch from the edge of the table in order of use, from the outside in. Diners begin using the cutlery farthest from the dinner plate and work inwards.

[4] Place the main-course knife on the right of the plate with the cutting edge facing to the left. If there is a fish course, the fish knife goes to the right of this.

[5] The forks go on the left of the plate. The salad fork is on the outside, followed by the main-course fork. If there is a dessert fork it may arrive with the dessert, or can be placed to the right of the main course fork or horizontally above the plate. All fork tines should face up.

[6] The soup spoon is placed to the right of the knives, or it may arrive with the soup course; the dessert spoon sits horizontally above the plate, pointing to the left. There may be a coffee spoon above the dessert fork.

[7] The bread-and-butter plate should sit at the ten o'clock position relative to the dinner plate, with the butter knife resting horizontally across the top of it.

[8] Glasses are placed above the plate to the right, again in order of use: the water glass should be about two inches above the knife; the red and white wine glasses are placed slightly below and to the right of the water glass; the champagne glass is placed to the far right.

TELL IF AN EGG IS FRESH

This is an easy method of checking how fresh your egg is, before you decide how best to use it, or indeed, whether to use it at all.

[1] First, check for a date stamp on your eggs. If you buy your eggs fresh from the free-range hen farm, consider asking your supplier to write the laying date on each egg. Even so, you would be advised to check for freshness: free-range hens don't always lay in the most obvious places. They may have been in the nest for a while before they were discovered.

[2] The rounded end of the egg contains a small air pocket when it is first laid. This pocket grows in size as the egg ages. Store eggs rounded side up in their carton in the refrigerator.

[3] Fill a bowl with cold water to a depth of a little more than the length of the egg.

[4] Gently place each egg into the water.

[5] A fresh egg will lie flat on the bottom of the bowl as there is insufficient air inside to lift it.

[6] The freshest eggs will fry the best, with a pert yolk and a white that will retain a tight shape.

[7] If the egg tilts upward slightly, but remains in the bottom of the bowl, it will be fresh enough to bake with.

[8] A less fresh egg will also remain on the bottom, but will stand in an upright position, bobbing up and down.

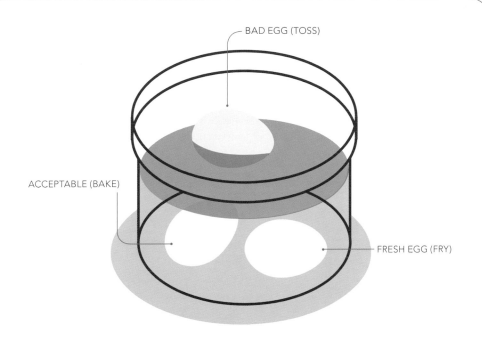

BAD EGG (TOSS)

ACCEPTABLE (BAKE)

FRESH EGG (FRY)

[9] Any eggs that have turned upright in the water will not be suitable for baking. As the strength of the whites will have begun to deteriorate, the yolk would collapse if you fried or poached it. Hence, reserve these eggs for scrambling and making omelets.

[10] An older egg, when hard-boiled, will have a dipped or flat end at the rounded end as a result of this expanded air pocket. Very fresh hard-boiled eggs are also very difficult to peel: at a week or so old, the shell will peel off far more easily.

[11] An egg that floats to the top of the bowl is a bad egg.

Here are the four basic ways of cooking an egg. (Boiled was just too easy to include!)

Fried Egg

Heat a tablespoon of oil in a heavy-based frying pan until it is hot but not smoking. Use very fresh eggs because they hold their shape better. Break the egg as close as you can to the pan without scalding yourself, to reduce the risk of the yolk breaking. Spoon oil over the top of the egg continually, avoiding the yoke if you like it very runny. When the whites are set and opaque the egg is ready to eat. The edge may be crispy and brown—if you don't want a crispy edge, use slightly cooler oil.

Poached Egg

The trick here is to add a little vinegar to the boiling water (about half a teaspoon per pint of water) and a pinch of salt. This increases the acidity and boiling temperature of the water, and makes the egg coagulate quickly before it has time to spread out and become straggly. Again, use very fresh eggs.

Crack the egg into a ladle or bowl then transfer it gently to a medium-sized pan containing about three inches of simmering water. Don't let the water boil too vigorously, as it will tear the egg into white shreds. Poach for three minutes until the whites are opaque and firm. Remove from the water with a slotted spoon.

Scrambled Egg

Break four large eggs into a bowl, whisk in four tablespoons of light cream, and season with salt and freshly ground black pepper. It is okay to use older eggs.

Melt a tablespoon of butter in a non-stick saucepan over a gentle heat until it foams, and allow it to cover the base of the pan. Add the eggs and wait for a few seconds. Then stir briskly with a wooden fork until three-quarters of the egg mixture has set. Remove from the heat and continue to stir until all the egg is creamy and glistening. Serve immediately.

Omelet

Cook one omelet at a time and use three eggs per omelet. Break the eggs into a bowl, season, and blend them gently with a fork for twenty seconds.

Melt a tablespoon of butter in a seven-inch non-stick omelet pan over a high heat. Make sure it coats the bottom and sides of the pan. Just before the butter begins to turn brown, add the egg and leave for a few seconds. Add filling now if required. Then, use a spatula to draw the egg from the edges into the center. Runny egg should flow in to fill the gap, so that within thirty seconds the whole omelet is ready to eat—soft and creamy with a frilly center. Fold over and serve immediately.

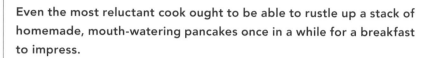

MAKE PANCAKES

Even the most reluctant cook ought to be able to rustle up a stack of homemade, mouth-watering pancakes once in a while for a breakfast to impress.

Basic Pancake Mix

To serve four (or two if you are very hungry) you will need:

Dry Ingredients:

1 cup all-purpose white flour
1 level tablespoon sugar
1 level teaspoon baking powder
Quarter teaspoon each of baking soda and salt

Wet Ingredients:

1 cup of milk or buttermilk
1 egg beaten until you can see soft bubbles
2 tablespoons oil or melted butter

Method

[1] First mix all the dry ingredients in a bowl. Sift in the flour from a little height, so that you add air into the mixture and make the pancakes that extra bit fluffy.

[2] Make a little "well" in the center of the dry mix.

[3] In a separate bowl, combine the eggs, milk, and oil or melted butter.

[4] Pour them into the well you made earlier in the center of the dry mix.

[5] Using a whisk or a fork, gradually combine the wet and the dry ingredients until you can no longer see any patches of dry mix left. If the mixture is slightly lumpy, it won't matter.

[6] The more you whisk the mixture, the thinner your pancakes will be. So don't over-whisk if you want to produce little plump pancakes. Likewise, this batter should not be made in advance and stored, as this will also make the pancakes thinner.

[7] Grease and heat a small, heavy griddle or frying pan. Drop a tiny amount of the mix into the center of the pan. If it bubbles, the pan is hot enough to cook with.

[8] Use about a half-cup of the batter per pancake. Wait until you begin to see the mixture bubbling, then turn it over and repeat the process on the other side.

Until you are ready to serve, you can keep the pancakes warm on a baking sheet in a moderate oven.

These pancakes should freeze quite well if you lay them between sheets of wax paper and placed inside air-tight freezer bags. Defrost thoroughly and wrap in foil before reheating at a gentle heat for about fifteen minutes.

Wherever possible, choose locally produced fruit that is in season. Out-of-season homegrown fruit, or imported fruit that is in season in its place of origin, contains less flavor and nutritional value than seasonal local produce.

Different fruits will indicate their ripeness in different ways.

Berry Fruits

Strawberries

Look for a bright red, shiny color and a firm texture. Choose small- to medium-sized fruit for maximum flavor.

Raspberries

Look for deep, rich-colored berries that are blemish-free and feel tender. They should look fat, dry, and clean.

Soft Summer Fruits

Apricots

Look for bright orange fruit that is juicy, plump, and has a little give in it when squeezed.

Bananas

Green bananas are under-ripe, but as they ripen easily in a brown paper bag along with an apple, this isn't necessarily a problem.

Cherries

Look for a deep, rich color and a smooth and shiny appearance.

Grapes

Look for bright fruit with green stems. They should look dry and plump.

Melon

Look for smooth skin that has some give to it at the stem end when squeezed and smells of melon up close.

Peaches

Look for fruit without green-colored skin that has some give in it when squeezed. You should be able to smell a peachy odor up close.

Plums

Look for a bright color and smooth skin that feels firm with a slight give to it.

Tropical Fruits

Avocados

Look for a shiny, deep, and even color, and some give to the fruit when squeezed. Do not choose fruit with black spots.

Mangoes

Look for fruit with few or no black spots and that have a slight give to them when squeezed. You should be able to smell mango from them up close.

Pineapples

Look for dark green leaves that come away from the fruit without any effort, and dry, firm skin that smells of pineapples.

Passion Fruit

Look for fruit that is wrinkly, not smooth and shiny, and that feels full and heavy.

Pawpaw/Papaya

Look for fruit that has some give in it at the stem end when squeezed. Do not choose fruit that has black spots.

Citrus Fruits

Grapefruits

Look for bright, heavy fruit with skin that feels thin, not thick.

Lemons

Look for bright, shiny skin that smells lemony up close.

Oranges

Look for bright orange skin that feels smooth and thin and is heavy to hold.

Chopping an onion is a mundane kitchen task, but many people make a bigger deal out of it than is strictly necessary. It needn't be an eye-watering experience if you follow these steps:

[1] Use a clean chopping board and a very sharp knife with a blade that is at least twice the length of the onion.

[2] Place the onion on the chopping board and cut it in half from root to stem.

[3] Cut off the stem and peel away the skin.

[4] To chop the onion roughly, cut off the root and simply make three or four vertical and horizontal cuts, leaving you with pieces of onion the size of your thumbnail. When holding the onion, curl the fingers with the fingernails facing the blade, to prevent injury.

[5] To dice the onion more finely, make straight vertical cuts along the ridges of the onion through one end and almost to the root end (this prevents the segments from falling apart). Then chop finely across the ridges and discard the root.

[6] If you don't want to use all of the onion, leave the outer skin intact on the leftovers and place in the refrigerator in a sealed bag or container. This will ensure it retains its moisture and prevent it from contaminating the contents of the refrigerator.

No tears

Chill the onion in the refrigerator before cutting.

The sharper the knife, the fewer tears. The sulfurous chemicals that irritate the eyes are caused by crushing and bruising rather than good sharp cutting.

Light a match halfway through the cutting process or place the chopping board alongside a flaming gas ring.

Breathe through your mouth.

Chew on some bread.

If none of the above works, wear swimming goggles!

Lobster is one of the most tasty and nutritious seafood delicacies. Not only is it packed with amino acids, A and B vitamins, and minerals such as potassium, magnesium, calcium, phosphorus, iron, and zinc, but lobster meat contains less fat than a skinless chicken breast. The only snag is how to eat it!

[1] Hold the lobster at the back and break off the legs one by one by twisting them gently at the joints. The meat can be removed by pulling the legs carefully through your clenched teeth.

[2] Now, remove the large front claws at the first joint by twisting them. Twist off the moveable part of the claw and peel away remaining pieces to reach the meat.

[3] Crack open the tip of the large part of the claw with a lobster-cracker or the back of a heavy chef's knife, and then push the meat out with a finger.

[4] Separate the tail section from the back by holding firmly in both hands and then bending it backward until it cracks.

[5] Remove the small flippers at the end of the tail in which there are small amounts of tasty meat.

[6] Most people consider the tail meat to be the tastiest part of the lobster. Push the meat out of the tail by sticking a fork through the flippers hole. Twist the fork while holding the tail with your other hand and the meat should come out in one piece. Carefully remove and discard the digestive tract (it looks like a black vein) and the stomach (which resembles a sack).

[7] More meat can be found in the hard body cavity. Cut it open between the walking legs and remove the meat from pockets just above where the legs join the body. In a female lobster you may even find some bright red roe – eggs—which can be eaten. The digestive system is green (when cooked) and is called the "tomalley." Some people consider this the best part of the whole lobster, while others consider it safer to avoid (there has been much concern about the level of toxins such as dioxin in the tomalley). It is commonly used it in sauces or lobster bisque soup.

No part of the lobster is actually harmful, but some parts should be avoided as they taste horrible (gills, stomach, intestine, eyes, antennae, antennules, and beak).

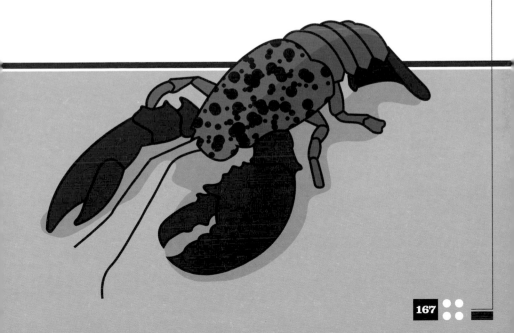

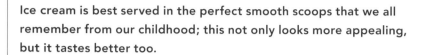

SCOOP ICE CREAM

Ice cream is best served in the perfect smooth scoops that we all remember from our childhood; this not only looks more appealing, but it tastes better too.

[1] Ice cream should be stored in a sealed container at between 0° and -5°F. Keep it in the part of the freezer which is always at a constant temperature. If the ice cream thaws and then refreezes because of temperature fluctuations, not only is it a health risk, but it also destroys the texture and makes crystals form.

[2] If the ice cream is too hard to scoop, leave it in the refrigerator until it softens slightly, or microwave it on high for about ten seconds.

[3] Buy a sturdy ice cream scoop with a solid and comfortable handle. You may have to use quite a lot of pressure to scoop up the ice cream, so you want a handle that you can grip comfortably.

[4] Scoops come in all shapes, sizes, and levels of technology, from simple stainless steel to durable acrylic. Some scoops (not metal) can be heated in the microwave (read the instructions on your scoop), while others have a built-in battery-powered heating mechanism. Spring-loaded scoops draw a blade around the inside of the scoop so that the ice cream falls away easily.

[5] If you are using a standard metal scoop, dip it in hot water just before scooping, then dry it quickly. The hot scoop will melt the ice cream, making it glide through more easily. Don't dip the wet scoop directly into the ice cream, as this will add water droplets to the container, and when it is replaced in the freezer, ice crystals will form.

[6] Bacteria can build up easily on a scoop even between servings, so make sure you clean it regularly in warm soapy water, rinse, and dry.

[7] Scoop in a circular motion, beginning at the edge of the container, and spiral inwards to the center.

[8] Ice cream is made by aerating cream; don't dig down too deeply under the surface—no more than about half an inch—otherwise you will compress the ice cream, changing both its texture and flavor.

[9] If you need to prepare a lot of scoops in advance for a party, dish them into a bowl, place it in the freezer, then remove when you are ready, separate the scoops, and serve.

Before learning how to use an espresso machine successfully, you need to know a perfect espresso when you are drinking one.

How Can You Tell A Perfect Espresso?

The aroma of a good espresso is unbeatable. More than any other coffee, espresso has a rich, intense coffee aroma due to the darker roast of the bean. The beautiful thick brown cream, known as the *crema*, is another reassuring sign. The *crema* locks in the aroma for longer and therefore intensifies it. The darker roast encourages the release of oils in the bean so that espresso has far more body than other coffees.

What Are The Essentials Of Making A Perfect Espresso?

[1] The grind of the coffee beans is key: if too fine, the espresso will have no *crema*; if too coarse, the taste will be bitter and it will pour through the machine too quickly to produce a *crema*. Ideally, the grind should be consistently gritty. If you have an automatic grinder, set it to a fine grind, though not the most fine.

[2] If you prefer to buy your beans ready ground, buy them in small quantities and seal them in an airtight container in the refrigerator, or even the freezer.

[3] The machine is the other determinant of a good espresso. Even the best domestic models will not be able to produce espresso of the quality you will enjoy at your nearest coffee house. However, as a basic guide, you need to invest in a machine that can reach temperatures of 194°F and pressurize the water to nine atmospheres or more.

[4] Ensure that you pack the coffee grounds firmly into the coffee basket of your machine, but do not over-pack as this will produce a bitter tasting espresso. The basket must be perfectly clean before use.

[5] If in doubt about the quality of your tap water, use cold bottled water, especially in hard water areas.

Using The Machine

[1] Ensure your machine is thoroughly cleaned and heated to the right temperature.

[2] Fill the water chamber with four tablespoons of water per cup.

[3] Check that you have fixed the boiler cap on tightly.

[4] Pack the coffee basket with two teaspoons of coffee grinds per cup and place the basket and the filter into the machine.

[5] Put a warmed cup in place and switch on the machine.

USE CHOPSTICKS

Chopsticks are traditionally used in China, Japan, Korea, and Vietnam. When eating in these countries or in a restaurant at home, bear in mind that using a knife and fork to eat this kind of food is like using a spoon to eat a burger. So take the time to learn how to use them correctly and politely. The mechanics and etiquette of chopsticks are of equal importance.

Mechanics

[1] Hold the thick end of the first chopstick gripped between your thumb and third finger, so that two or three inches of the thin end stick out beyond your fingertips.

[2] Hold the second chopstick rather like you would hold a pencil, using the tip of your thumb to hold it against your index finger.

[3] Press the two ends against your plate until they line up. Now pick up your food by pivoting the top stick only, while the second stick remains anchored below.

[4] Don't grip too hard or eating will become an uncomfortable experience as your hand will quickly begin to ache.

Etiquette

[1] Do not eat directly from a communal dish. Transfer a morsel to your own plate first, using the thick end of the sticks.

[2] Do not point your sticks at anyone or gesticulate with them.

[3] Do not lay your chopsticks down on your plate. When not being used they should be placed on the table with the tips parallel (not crossed) on a chopstick rest, and pointing to the left.

[4] Do not leave your chopsticks stuck into your food, especially rice (this is only done at funerals).

[5] It is rude to rummage around a communal plate searching out the best bits. Choose food from the top of the dish. Dithering around indecisively with your sticks hovering over plates of food while you choose is also considered rude.

[6] Do not pass food from your chopsticks to those of another person (another funerary practice).

[7] Do not reach over someone else with your chopsticks.

[8] Avoid spearing food. If a morsel is too big to eat, cut it by trapping it between the ends of the chopsticks and perform a scissor action while applying pressure.

[9] Do not lower your head to get closer to the bowl. Instead, lift the bowl to your chest and then eat.

[10] It is acceptable to make slurping noises while eating, but avoid making noise with your chopsticks (e.g., clicking them together), and never suck or lick them clean.

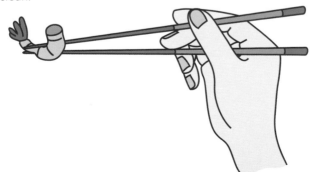

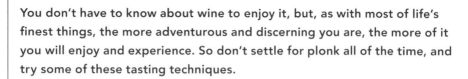

TASTE WINE

You don't have to know about wine to enjoy it, but, as with most of life's finest things, the more adventurous and discerning you are, the more of it you will enjoy and experience. So don't settle for plonk all of the time, and try some of these tasting techniques.

[1] Pour the wine into a clean, dry, uncolored glass at room temperature. Warm, dirty, dusty, or poorly rinsed glasses will affect the taste of the wine.

[2] Do not overfill the glass; ideally it should be no more than half full. Leave plenty of room at the top of the glass to aerate the wine and trap the aroma.

[3] Hold the glass by the stem. If you hold the bowl of the glass, the heat from your hand can adversely affect the flavor of the wine by changing its temperature.

[4] Appreciate the color and clarity of the wine by holding the glass against a white background in a well-lit place. White wines grow darker and more golden with age. Red wines begin life as bright or purple red, and opaque, and mellow into a rich tawny color with age.

[5] Swirl the wine around the glass to mix it with the air. This enables the wine to release some of its smell ("bouquet").

[6] Notice how much of the wine sticks to the side of the bowl. If a wine has "legs," it will leave a trace on the side, which is a sign that it is full-bodied. Younger and thinner wines have little to no legs.

[7] Stick your nose into the top of the bowl and take a good sniff. Pay attention to the many accents—black currants, raspberries, oak, leather, cinnamon, apples, earth, old socks. If the wine smells musty it is "corked"—it has reacted with the cork and gone bad.

[8] Take a sip and allow the wine to swirl around your mouth. There are taste buds all over your tongue that can detect different aspects of the taste. You'll taste sweetness in the middle of the tongue and acidity on the sides and back of the throat. However, most of the taste will actually be provided by your sense of smell.

[9] Now watch out for the aftertaste ("finish"). This is how the wine feels in your mouth and nose after you have swallowed it (or traditionally spat it out).

It is a common misconception that the characteristic "pop" you get from uncorking champagne is desirable. It isn't. That's the sound of too many precious bubbles escaping. Follow the instructions below to produce the perfect glass of bubbly.

[1] Warm champagne will foam hopelessly, no matter how carefully you uncork it. Make sure you chill the bottle for about twenty minutes in a bucket of ice before opening.

[2] Remove the bottle from the ice bucket and dry it off with a clean towel.

[3] Unpeel the foil a little so that you can see some of the cork.

[4] Carefully unscrew the little wire handle at the side of the cage that covers the cork, so that the cage is loose.

[5] Remove the cage if you wish, although it is not necessary, and you may risk the cork popping before you are ready.

[6] Cover the end of the bottle with the towel, making sure your hand and fingers are firmly holding the cork through the towel.

[7] Point the bottle away from other people and any delicate items, just in case the uncorking doesn't go according to plan.

[8] Support the bottle by its neck with your free hand.

[9] Gently turn the cork until you begin to feel it loosen.

[10] Keeping a tight hold on the cork with one hand (through the towel), gently turn the bottle, not the cork, with the other hand.

[11] You need to listen for a gentle sigh, or a "hiss," as the cork is very slowly released from the neck of the bottle.

[12] Remove the towel and the cork, and you are ready to pour.

Serving Champagne

[1] Don't wait for a special occasion. Champagne is good to drink any time.

[2] Serve in tall champagne flutes.

[3] Hold the glass at a slight angle, and pour the champagne slowly, aiming at the inside edge of the glass. Fill each glass no more than two-thirds full.

[4] Remember that your fingers should hold a champagne glass by the stem, not the bowl, so that you do not warm the drink.

[5] Champagne tastes great with fruit or shellfish, especially oysters.

[6] Keep the bottle on ice while you are drinking it.

Pouring a beer with a perfect head of foam can be a complicated process for the uninitiated. A good head releases the full aroma and looks more inviting, so that your taste buds will be salivating in anticipation and your enjoyment heightened.

Choosing Your Beer

There are bars across the U.S. and Europe that boast hundreds of different beers. What could be better than to spend some time researching in one of them? When it comes to home enjoyment, experimentation is the key. Just one golden rule: buy and consume only the freshest beer. Any left on the shelf for too long will have begun to lose flavor already.

Choosing The Right Glass

This is an important part of the process. Most European beers come with their own specifically designed glasses that go a long way to maximizing both the head and the aroma of the beer. It is worth researching your favorite beers to discover whether the brewers have designed any glassware.

Alternatively, the basic prerequisite is that your beer glass curves in slightly at the top, which will encourage a good head and will retain as much of the aroma as possible.

Pouring The Beer

[1] Wash the glass thoroughly to remove anything that may impair the beer, or its ability to support a good head of foam.

[2] The glass should not be chilled in a refrigerator, as serving a beer that is too cold will inhibit both flavor and aroma.

[3] Hold the glass at a forty-five-degree angle to the beer.

[4] Pour from a height, aiming for a point midway up the sloped side of the glass.

[5] Once the glass is about half full, turn it upright.

[6] Still pouring from a height, now aim for the dead center of the beer in the glass. This will begin to build up the head.

[7] The head should just bob over the rim of the glass, and should be about an inch or so deep.

[8] The full impact of the hops flavor in the beer is found in the head. This is worth bearing in mind if it is this flavor you most enjoy, in which case you may wish to try for a deeper head through which to drink.

MAKE A PERFECT BLOODY MARY

The Bloody Mary has become a cocktail of legendary status. First mixed in the 1920s at Harry's Bar in Paris, it made Ernest Hemingway an enthusiastic devotee. The market is now flooded with prepared Bloody Mary mixes to which you simply add vodka, but these are a very poor substitute for making this classic drink from scratch.

What's In A Name?

The world of classic mixed drinks, or cocktails, is a highly evocative one, not least because of their alluring names. The Harvey Wallbanger, the Manhattan, and the Daiquiri have echoes of 1940s chic. The origins of the name "Bloody Mary" have been subject to some dispute. Some claim the name has great historical reference: Mary Tudor first earned the nickname after having countless English Protestants executed during her brief reign in the fifteenth century. Anecdotal history has it that a customer at Harry's Bar in the 1920s said the drink reminded him of a woman called Mary he had once met at the Bucket of Blood club in Chicago. And so a legend began.

What You Will Need

An old fashioned cocktail glass
A cocktail shaker
An airtight container
An ounce and a half of vodka
Three ounces of tomato juice
The juice of half a lemon
A dash of Tabasco sauce

A dash of Worcestershire sauce
Celery salt
Salt
Pepper
A garnish of your choice: a celery stalk, olives, a wedge of lime, shrimp

Method

The "perfect" Bloody Mary is of course highly subjective. The key is to establish the balance of ingredients that is perfect for you. The basic quantities of vodka, tomato juice, and lemon juice are more or less a requirement. The definition of a "dash" is where you will need to experiment. The starting point is to go with a quarter-of-a-teaspoon as a basic guide. However, some aficionados will insist upon more precise measurements, classically three drops of Tabasco and seven of Worcestershire.

Whatever precise ingredients you decide upon, the art is in the mixing. Begin by pouring the vodka into a cocktail shaker pre-filled with ice. Then add the tomato juice, Worcestershire sauce, Tabasco, and a pinch each of salt, pepper, and celery salt. Stir or shake vigorously.

The mix will keep in an airtight container in the refrigerator for up to four weeks and will improve with age. When you are ready to drink, pour into your glass over ice and garnish.

Prevention is always the best cure. Drinking responsibly eliminates the need for hangover cures, but if you have overindulged, there are several precautions that will mitigate the damage to brain and body.

[1] Don't drink on an empty stomach. Food helps to soak up alcohol so that it is absorbed into your bloodstream slowly.

[2] Stick to one drink. Mixing drinks is a surefire way to wake up with a thick head. A drink contains a lot of chemicals, other than alcohol. These are added for taste and color and are called congeners. Mixing them together creates a chemical cocktail which puts a lot of strain on your liver, but your own liver produces by far the most toxic substance as it tries to break down the alcohol.

[3] When your liver breaks down the alcohol, the first substance it produces is acetaldehyde, which is more toxic than alcohol and is actually a component of embalming fluid. If you drink too quickly your liver can't process the alcohol quickly enough, and instead of being converted into harmless acetic acid, the excess acetaldehyde ends up in the bloodstream, causing cell damage (even DNA damage), and nasty hangover symptoms such as increased heart rate, headache, and nausea. Drink more slowly and be kind to your liver.

[4] Light-colored drinks tend to cause less of a hangover than dark drinks. For instance, white wine or vodka is kinder than red wine or port, because the latter contain more chemicals. Cheap wine is worse for you than good-quality wine.

[5] Alternate your drinks throughout the night—have one soft drink for every alcoholic one. Not only will you consume less alcohol, you will also drink more water.

[6] Before you go to bed, drink three pints of water.

[7] After a night's drinking you may be feeling hungry. It's actually a good idea to eat a little before bedtime, as long as you avoid sugary foods and choose those that will release their energy slowly through the night—protein, fatty foods, citrus and succulent fruits (not bananas), and vegetables.

[8] Alcohol makes you urinate water-soluble vitamins, so take a multi-vitamin before you go to sleep. Avoid painkillers.

[9] In the morning, if possible, stay in bed, drink lots of water, and avoid caffeinated drinks such as coffee or colas, which will dehydrate you.

[10] Stay cool. Hangover sweats are caused by alcohol interfering with your body's ability to control its temperature.

[11] Eat food with a low glycemic index, little and often, and avoid sugary foods. Stay off alcohol for a few days.

SMOKE A CIGAR

To the uninitiated, knowing how to choose, cut, light, and smoke a cigar can be a daunting prospect.

Choosing The Right Cigar For You

The shorter and fatter the cigar, the hotter the smoke is going to be. If you are new to cigar smoking, you will do better to select a long, narrow cigar.

Cutting The Cigar

The open end of the cigar is the end you light. The end you smoke is closed with a cap that you need to cut off before you can smoke. This needs to be done with care so as to avoid tearing the wrapping around the tobacco. Use a guillotine, a double-bladed cigar cutter, for this purpose, and make the cut at the point at which the cap and the wrapper meet. You need to leave about an eighth-of-an-inch of the cap on the cigar in order to keep the wrapper securely in place.

Lighting The Cigar

Lighting a cigar will take a lot longer than lighting a cigarette. Ideally, you need to invest in a proper cigar lighter, as the sulfur from matches will spoil the taste of the cigar. The key point to bear in mind is that you do not set light to the cigar: you merely singe the ends of it in order to heat it up. You need to wait until you see embers. Hold the cigar at no more than a thirty-degree angle; any more than this and you risk the whole thing going up in flames. Never use a candle, as the wax will ruin the cigar. Once the cigar is lit, you will need to give a few gentle puffs and check that it is *evenly* lit.

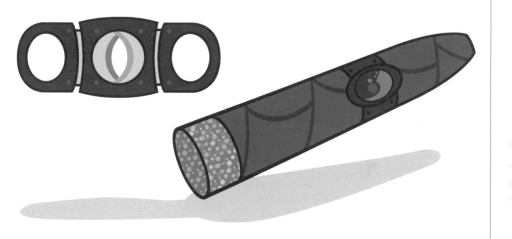

Smoking The Cigar

Smoke the cigar slowly, taking one or two puffs a minute. Any faster and the cigar will be too hot and taste bitter. Never inhale the smoke, just draw on it gently.

It is generally considered pretentious to keep the band on. Wait until you have had a dozen or so puffs and remove it carefully. (Don't attempt to un-peel it before then: the glue will rip the wrapper.)

Finally, don't tap the ash off the cigar as a build up of ash will cool the cigar down. A cigar that retains a tower of ash is a cigar of quality.

Step One. Why Do You Want To Quit?

This is the easy bit: we all know why. But research shows that if you really believe smoking will harm you or a loved one, you are more likely to quit for good.

Step Two. How Are You Going To Quit?

This will depend on a host of factors.

1. How much do you smoke in a day?

2. How long have you been smoking?

3. Do you have a track record of trying to quit?

4. Do you have strong cravings at certain times of the day?

Depending on the answers to these questions, you may decide to go right ahead and smoke your last cigarette, then throw the rest away and go cold turkey. Or you may decide to cut down gradually first; reducing the number you smoke little by little until you phase them out altogether. Finally, if you have a strong addiction, you may wish to try nicotine replacement therapy.

Whichever you decide, you need to make it very public that you intend to quit.

And get rid of temptation: lighters, matches, and ashtrays, as well as the cigarettes themselves. Launder your clothes to get rid of the smell of cigarettes. If certain people, places or situations trigger your desire for a cigarette, avoid them for a while, until your resolve is stronger.

Step Three. Picking Your Quit Date.

Again, make this public. Tell friends and colleagues. Make a wager with some-one to help you make it through the day. Fill your bag, pockets, and desk drawers with easy substitutes: gum, candy, etc.

Step Four. Getting Through Your Quit Day.

Fill your day and keep busy. Clean the floor, tidy up a closet, anything; just keep busy. Avoid alcohol, but drink lots of fluids, including plenty of water, to flush out the toxins from your body. Your body begins its recovery from the effects of nicotine within hours of your last cigarette.

Feel a craving coming on? Fight the urge. Take a good deep breath. Set yourself a ten-minute activity—anything from running up and down a flight of stairs to going out to mail a letter. Most importantly, put off the act of light-ing up.

Step Five. Thought Quit Day was tough? "Staying quit" is the real challenge

Start recognizing what a major achievement quitting is. Why not put aside your cigarette money so that you can save up for a real treat to reward your-self with? Remind yourself how well you are doing and fight the urge to smoke just one cigarette. Take a deep breath and hold firm.

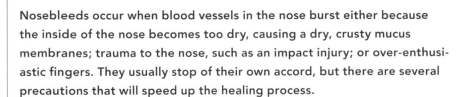

STOP A NOSEBLEED

Nosebleeds occur when blood vessels in the nose burst either because the inside of the nose becomes too dry, causing a dry, crusty mucus membranes; trauma to the nose, such as an impact injury; or over-enthusiastic fingers. They usually stop of their own accord, but there are several precautions that will speed up the healing process.

[1] Stay calm. If you become agitated, your blood pressure will increase and prolong the bleeding. Sit down and tilt your head forward to prevent blood from running down you throat. (Leaning backward doesn't help; it just makes you swallow blood.)

[2] Use your thumb and forefinger to pinch the nose and apply pressure to the nasal septum (the piece of cartilage which runs through the middle of the nose) for up to fifteen minutes. Breathe through your mouth.

[3] Crush some ice in a dishtowel and press it against the nose.

[4] Don't wedge tissues up your nose to stem the flow, as this will increase nasal pressure and may cause further damage.

[5] Soak a small wedge of tissue and place it between your top lip and gum, then compress your lip over the wedge.

If your nose continues to bleed for more than fifteen minutes, seek medical help immediately.

After The Nosebleed Has Stopped

[1] Spray a fine mist of water into the air and breathe it in. This helps to moisten the mucus membranes in cases where the nosebleed has been caused by hot, dry air.

[2] Avoid the temptation to pick out the clotted blood inside the nose. Allow a few hours for the nasal tissues to heal. Also, avoid blowing your nose.

[3] Avoid any activity that raises your heartbeat or blood pressure, such as strenuous exercise or heavy lifting, for at least twenty-four hours.

[4] If you lie down, prop yourself up with pillows to ensure that your head is higher than your heart; this will decrease nasal pressure.

Stings and bruises are always painful and unsightly, but early intervention can reduce the effects and speed up the healing process.

Stings

[1] Remove the stinger as quickly and as carefully as possible, ensuring that you don't leave any part of it embedded in your skin. The quicker you remove the stinger, the less venom will enter your body.

[2] The best way to remove a stinger is to scrape it with the edge of something, like a blunt knife or a fingernail. Don't squeeze the stinger out as you might remove a thorn, because this could force more venom out into the wound.

[3] Wash the sting area with soap and warm water, to reduce the risk of infection, and to remove venom at the surface.

[4] Apply sting cream, or make up your own itch-reducing paste by mixing a little baking soda with water, until you can visit a pharmacist. You can also apply a cold compress to reduce swelling. (Don't use ice directly on the affected area.)

[5] Don't scratch. Instead, some people recommend lightly tapping the sting area to spread the venom over a wider area and reduce the itching.

[6] If you have a history of allergic reactions to stings, or suffer excessively painful or pronounced swelling, or any symptoms other than localized pain (e.g., shortness of breath, nausea, burning, body rash), seek medical assistance immediately.

Bruises

A bruise is caused by damage to tiny blood vessels underneath your skin. Most bruises will disappear within a few weeks, but there are a few things you can do to help.

[1] Apply a cold compress (crushed ice in a bag or towel or a cold soda can). This constricts the blood vessels and reduces the blood flow to the damaged area. Keeping the area raised also reduces the blood flow. Don't waste a good steak by holding it against a black eye. It is the coldness of the meat that is effective, nothing else.

[2] Anti-bruising preparations, such as a Vitamin K cream, can be applied to the site, and herbs such as witch hazel and homeopathic remedies are also effective. Always read the instructions of whatever you use.

[3] Some bruises cause complications and require medical assistance. Some bruises become firm and larger over time (called a hematoma) rather than shrinking. A rarer complication occurs when the body deposits calcium in the bruise site, making it tender and firm (called heterotopic ossification). If in doubt, see a doctor.

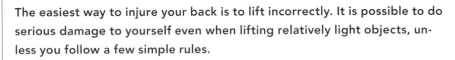

The easiest way to injure your back is to lift incorrectly. It is possible to do serious damage to yourself even when lifting relatively light objects, unless you follow a few simple rules.

[1] Evaluate whether the object is too awkward a shape or too heavy for you to lift on your own, and get someone to help you if necessary. If two or more people are lifting, one person should be in charge and only that person should give commands. Be aware of the balance of the object—one part may be much heavier than another.

[2] Know beforehand where you intend to carry the object, and check the route for obstacles—uneven flooring, wet and slippery patches, closed doors, and other hazards.

[3] Make sure that the object is securely packaged, otherwise it may slip from your grip, or slip out of its packaging, causing injury to you and damage to the object.

[4] Bend at the knees while keeping your back straight (*i.e.*, in line with your head and pelvis). Use slow and smooth movements and avoid sudden or jerky movements. The object should be comfortably within your control at all times.

[5] Grip the object firmly using your whole hand (not just the tips of your fingers).

[6] Keep the object close to your body. Over-reaching is another common cause of injury.

[7] Rise to a standing position by straightening your knees. Tuck in your chin to ensure correct alignment of your neck, because your upper back is as vulnerable to injury as your lumbar region.

[8] While carrying the object to its final position, keep your body aligned, and avoid twisting to the side. Keep your shoulders squared with your hips at all times. Turn by moving your feet rather than your upper body.

[9] If you are carrying anything over a long distance, take frequent breaks. Keep your head up and look ahead.

[10] Lower the object the same way you lifted it, by bending your legs and keeping your back straight. If you need to adjust the position precisely, set it down first, then make slight adjustments.

[11] If you are spending several hours doing a lot of lifting, perform stretching and relaxation exercises frequently to allow your back and arms to lengthen, and to recover from the stress of lifting.

PERFORM CPR

CPR stands for "cardiopulmonary resuscitation" and is a combination of artificial respiration and chest compressions that is given to victims in cardiac arrest (*i.e.*, when the heart stops pumping blood). CPR buys a little extra time by supplying the brain and other vital organs with enough oxygen to survive until the paramedics arrive. Many institutions offer basic classes in CPR, and only those trained should attempt it.

Don't perform CPR on unconscious persons who are breathing unaided and have a pulse. Place them in the recovery position that ensures they maintain an open airway, can't swallow their tongue, and won't choke on their own vomit.

Ensure the person is lying on the side, supported by one leg and one arm. Keep the airway open by tilting the head and lifting the chin.

If the airway is not open and the person is not breathing, begin resuscitation mindful of the ABCs of critical care: A-airway. B-breathing. C-circulation.

Airway

[1] To open the airway, lift the chin with one hand, while pushing down on the forehead with the other to tilt the head back.

[2] Once the airway is open, look for chest movement and listen and feel for breathing by placing an ear close to the person's mouth.

Breathing

If opening the airway does not cause the person to begin to breathe spontane-
ously, artificial respiration must be started:

[1] Tilt the person's head back, lift up the chin, and pinch the nostrils together.

[2] Take a deep breath and seal your mouth over the other person's mouth.

[3] Breathe slowly into the person's mouth, and check that the person's
chest rises.

[4] Repeat until the person starts breathing or until assistance arrives.

Circulation

If there is no heart beat and no pulse (*i.e.*, no circulation), phone 911 for adults before commencing CPR. For children under age eight, do one minute of CPR before calling 911, then continue CPR.

[1] Place the heel of one hand on the middle half of the person's breast-bone, and the heel of the other hand on top of the first.

[2] Lock the fingers.

[3] Keeping elbows straight, press downward firmly and quickly with hands then relax and repeat compression. Press down approximately two inches.

[4] The rate of compression for victims age eight or older should be approximately one hundred compressions per minute. Do fifteen compressions, and then give artificial respiration twice. Repeat until assistance arrives.

[5] For children under age eight, do five chest compressions followed by one breath and repeat.

The basics of pitching are grip, balance, direction, and concentration. Warm up and stretch thoroughly beforehand.

[1] Special grips are used for curve balls and other specialty pitches, but for a basic throw, grip with your middle three fingers over the top of the ball, perpendicular to the seams at their widest point, with your thumb on the bottom of the ball. The ball should not be touching the palm of your hand. Fold your pinkie into your palm.

[2] Stand sideways to your target with your feet wider than shoulder-width apart, and your head facing the target. You must keep one foot on the rubber (on top of the pitcher's mound) during the pitch, and you can only take one step forward.

[3] Wind up by lifting and bending your front leg off the ground in a knee-to-chest action, without changing your center of gravity (your head should stay at the same level during the entire pitch).

[4] From your position of balance, take a stride forward while your throwing arm goes backward to get into a high cocked or L-position. The throwing hand should be at its highest point when your foot hits the ground. As soon as the lead foot is planted, twist the upper body to face the target and bring the throwing arm forward, keeping your head parallel to the mound at all times.

[5] Don't push forward with the back foot, but lead with your lower body to transfer rotational movement into throwing speed. Your elbow should be at shoulder height.

[6] Snap your wrist as the ball leaves your hand—thumb first, followed by fingertips.

[7] After releasing the ball from your fingertips, follow through by bringing your arm down and across your body.

[8] If you want to throw faster, move faster and practice throwing balls. Fast pitching is not about spending hours in the weight room developing arm strength, but a combination of strength built through throwing, and increasing rotational body and arm speed.

After the pitch, stay facing the plate. Stay balanced and be prepared to field the ball.

SHOOT A FREE THROW IN BASKETBALL

A free throw is a clear, unguarded shot made from the free throw line, which is fifteen feet from the hoop. Basketball games are won and lost on free throws, which are one of the most vital parts of a team's arsenal.

[1] Stand just behind the free throw line with your feet parallel and shoulder-width apart, with your upper body squared toward the basket. Every free throw line has a little hole or nail right in the middle, in line with the middle of the rim. Use this point to ensure you stand in exactly the same place every time.

[2] Relax and take a few deep breaths to keep you calm. Bounce the ball a few times if it helps to get you into your rhythm and stops you from thinking too much. Try to develop a routine to use before every free throw. In a stressful situation a little pre-throw ritual will keep you calm, loose, and focused.

[3] While supporting the ball lightly with your non-shooting hand, place your shooting hand on the ball so that your middle three fingers are on the seams, with your thumb and palm supporting the ball.

[4] Keep your shooting forearm straight and pointing toward the basket, and keep your elbow tucked in and in line with the basket.

[5] Aim to shoot the ball just above the rim of the basket. Look at the back of the rim. If you focus on the front of the rim you risk shooting too short.

[6] Your arms do the supporting and aiming, while your legs should provide most of the momentum to propel the ball. So bend your knees and then straighten them again to give you the vertical spring into the shot.

[7] Flick your wrist forward and release the ball in a fluid motion with your fingertips. This causes backspin and allows greater control.

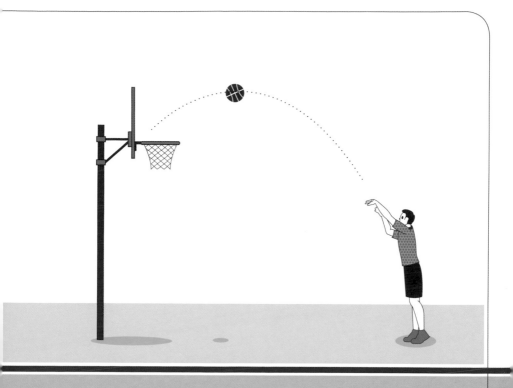

[8] Follow through with both arms and continue to reach for the rim with your shooting arm. Your shooting hand should end the shot bent forward at the wrist.

Practice shooting free throws when you are tired, because that's how you'll be during a game. Shooting when you're fresh doesn't match the game situation.

Free throws are a mental challenge. On bad shots your mind often gets in the way of your technique. Believe you can do it, block out any bad thoughts, and concentrate on sinking the shot.

Hitting a golf ball is easy, but hitting it effectively is a much greater challenge. Here are the basics of driving and putting.

The Drive

Address the ball

Stand with both feet together facing the ball, about three-quarters of an arm's-length away from it. Then, take a small step toward the target with your left foot and step backward with your right foot, so that your feet are a shoulder's-width apart. Your hands should be slightly ahead of the ball.

The swing

Think of swinging the club smoothly and letting the ball get in the way. A swing is composed of the backswing, swing, and follow through, but it forms one single, smooth unit (don't pause at the top of your backswing).

The target

As you swing, keep your head still and your eyes fixed on the ball. To make the ball go up, you have to think of hitting down. Do not think about scooping the ball upwards. Think of the fairway or flag as your target, rather than the ball.

Body weight

At the beginning of the swing your weight is evenly balanced between the heels and toes of both feet; at the top of the backswing, about three-quarters of your weight is on your back foot. By impact, about three-quarters of your weight will have been transferred to your front foot, and at the end of the follow-through about ninety percent of your weight should be on the outside of your front foot.

The Putt

Establish the line of the ball by standing behind it, and putt with your head as far behind the ball as comfortably possible. Weight should be evenly balanced.

Take several practice strokes standing next to the ball.

Keep the face of the putter square to the line at all times.

Instead of trying to sink the ball in the hole, concentrate on getting the ball as close to the hole as possible. This will help you to stay loose and relaxed. Concentrate on the speed of the ball and the line it will follow.

Think of your arms and shoulder as a triangle and the stroke as a pendulum. As you strike the ball solidly with the middle of the clubface, keep your head down and focus on the ball, rather than look up to see where it went.

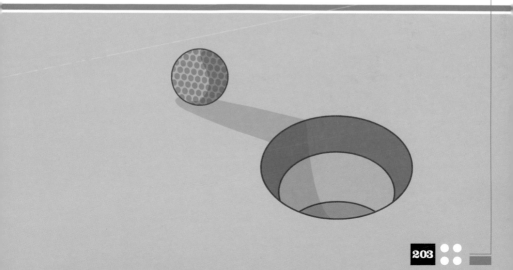

As well as being a fun, healthy form of exercise, swimming is important because it helps to keep you safe. When people can't swim, not only do they feel uncomfortable around water, they are also a potential risk to the safety of those around them. Here are two of the most common swimming strokes explained.

Breaststroke

The breaststroke is the slowest swimming stroke, but when it is performed with the correct technique it is nevertheless powerful, smooth, and impressive.

[1] The key to an effective breaststroke is keeping your body level at the surface of the water by keeping your shoulders in line and your hips flat.

[2] Forward motion is generated by alternating between kicking with the legs, stretching the whole body, then pulling back and round with the arms.

[3] The legs move like those of a frog. Bend both knees and lift them toward your bottom, with your feet slightly apart.

[4] At the top of the lift, turn your feet so they are perpendicular to your legs, and then quickly push out and slightly down with your feet.

[5] Bring your legs together again; squeeze the water and point your toes as your knees touch. When you are confident with the kick, speed it up and try to turn it into a whipping action. Don't make the kick too wide—it should be a little outside your body width—otherwise it will slow you down.

[6] Immediately after the kick, stretch your arms straight out in front of you just under the water surface so that your whole body is long and thin and you glide for a moment. Put your face in the water as you stretch.

[7] Then turn both hands outward and draw a powerful horizontal circle making sure your hands stay in front of your shoulders and that you can see them at all times.

[8] As your arms pull, raise your chest and lift your shoulders out of the water. Bend your elbows as you make the circle, then tuck them into your chest before shooting them forward again into the stretch.

[9] Breathe in as you complete the circle and breathe out when your head is under the water.

[10] The whole motion goes like this: kick, stretch-glide, arms and repeat.

[11] When you have mastered the mechanics, you can increase your speed even more by undulating your body in the water. Dive down and then lift your shoulders out of the water, so that your body moves forward in a series of smooth curves rather than straight line. If your shoulders are raised properly, you can kick downward more with your feet, so long as your legs come back to the surface for the stretch-glide.

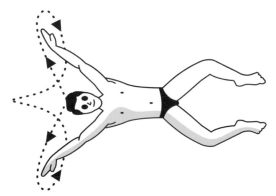

Front Crawl

This can be a difficult stroke to master, but is the easiest and fastest swimming stroke once you know how.

How to lie in the water

[1] Keep your body flat and level, close to the surface of the water.

[2] Your face should be flat in the water until you come up for breath, held as straight and still as you can manage.

[3] As you come up for breath, turn your head to the side rather than jerk it backward out of the water.

[4] Keep your head facing the bottom of the pool in a straight line with your body, but try to look ahead of you with your eyes.

[5] Try to build up a rhythmic breathing pattern, blowing out a good strong breath into the water first.

[6] Aim to breathe every two or three strokes, and experiment with turning to the left and right to breathe to see which suits you better.

The legs

[1] Kick your whole leg, not just from the the knee down.

[2] Keep your knees slightly bent and kick from the top of your leg as fast as you can.

[3] The legs need to stay close together at all times so that they keep you as streamlined as possible. Therefore you need to kick fast and shallow, making a tiny splash as you do so.

[4] Your feet should almost touch each other as you kick.

[5] Your legs will need to kick a little less vigorously if you wish to use the front crawl to cover longer distances.

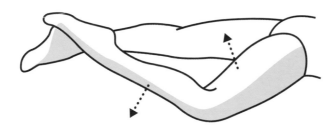

The arms

[1] Bring one arm into the water with as little splash as possible.

[2] Cut into the water smoothly, thumb first.

[3] Bend your elbow as it travels through the water, and keep working your arm until it is back at your thigh.

[4] Bring the arm up and out of the water smoothly and stretch it out in front of you again, alternating all these movements between both arms.

[5] The more energy you put into bending your elbow and pulling your arm down through the water, the more speed you will generate.

[6] Be careful not to over-stretch your arm as you lift it out of the water. Keep it low as you reach over, and you will lose less power.

[7] As you pull down through the water, bend your elbow up a little, so that it just lifts clear of the water.

[8] Keep your arm close to your body as you move it through the water.

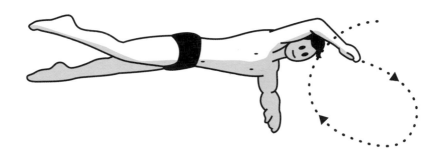

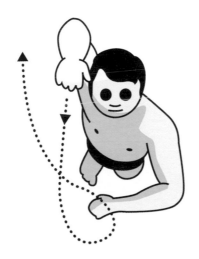

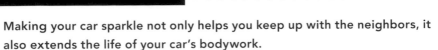
Making your car sparkle not only helps you keep up with the neighbors, it also extends the life of your car's bodywork.

[1] Choose a spot away from direct sunlight; otherwise the soap will dry before you have a chance to rinse it off.

[2] Close the doors and make sure all the windows are shut tight.

[3] Fill a bucket with warm water and add car shampoo as directed on the bottle (never use detergent, which attacks the rubber and vinyl fittings, seals, windshield wiper blades, etc).

[4] Using a hose, or power washer, give the car a thorough dousing, starting with the roof and working down. Remove as much caked on mud and dirt as you can. The more grit you can get rid of at this stage, the smaller the risk of making tiny scratches in the paint-work with the sponge.

[5] Power washers are ideal for attacking stubborn dirt and dried-on bugs, but beware of getting too close with them, or you might remove more than you bargained for. Start about eight feet from your car and move closer until you have a good sense of the water-power.

[6] Hose under the trim and wheel arches, where lots of mud collects.

[7] Soak a clean sponge in the bucket and clean the roof. Then wash one side at a time, working downward, rinsing and soaking the sponge regularly in the bucket. Don't clean the wheels or hubcaps yet. Hose off the first side before the soap dries (as always, start at the top and work down), then sponge-wash

the trunk, and hose off. Now wash the other side, and hose. Finally, clean the windshield and hood, and then hose them off. Hosing regularly prevents the suds from drying out and minimizes streaking.

[8] Now wash the wheels using a separate sponge or alloy brush. This is an area where lots of dust and grit collects, so it should be washed last to keep the water clean and grit-free. Hose off the wheels.

[9] Remove all excess water and streaks by rubbing the car all over with a chamois leather ("shammy").

[10] Apply a non-abrasive wax to the paint-work and windows (not the windshield) with a damp cloth, using small circular movements. Work on a small section at a time until you have covered all the bodywork. Do not wax the door seals or vinyl bumpers. When the wax has dried, buff to a shine with a clean cloth.

[11] If you are a buff lover, repeat step 9 to apply a second coat of wax and achieve an even deeper protective shine.

[12] If you want to drive away immediately, check your brakes—they may still be wet.

JUMP-START A VEHICLE

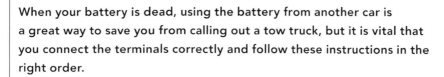

When your battery is dead, using the battery from another car is a great way to save you from calling out a tow truck, but it is vital that you connect the terminals correctly and follow these instructions in the right order.

[1] Do not jump-start your engine if the battery is frozen, the battery casing is cracked, or the battery has been unused for several days (there may be a build-up of flammable hydrogen gas).

[2] Batteries contain sulfuric acid, so you must protect your hands and eyes by wearing goggles and gloves. If you get any acid on your eyes or skin, wash immediately with lots of water and seek medical help. Keep well away from open flames and do not smoke, as batteries can release flammable and explosive gases.

[3] Before you begin, make sure the batteries are the same voltage (it should be printed on the top of the casing). Also, check the cable connectors on the dead battery; if they are damaged, corroded, or worn, this alone may be the reason the car won't start, and jump-starting will be ineffective.

[4] Park the source vehicle (the car that is working correctly) close to the dead one, but do not let them touch. Turn off both ignitions and apply the emergency brakes of both cars.

[5] Connect the positive terminal (marked POS or +) on the dead battery to the positive terminal on the source battery with the red jump lead.

[6] Connect the black jump lead to the negative terminal (marked NEG or -) of the source battery and attach the other end to the engine block of the dead car, as far away from the dead battery as possible.

[7] Do not allow the black and red clamps to touch each other, and keep the jump leads away from moving engine parts, such as the fan belt.

[8] Everyone should stand well away from the two cars, with the exception of the two drivers.

[9] Start the engine of the source car, and then attempt to start the dead car. If it doesn't start immediately, wait ten seconds and try again. If it still fails to start after repeated attempts, stop, or you may damage the starter motor.

[10] If the car starts, keep the engine running. Remove the cable clips in the reverse order: grounding clamp first, then the clip from the NEG terminal of the source battery, followed by the red cable ends.

[11] Do not turn off the engine of the jump-started car until you reach your destination. When you get home, recharge the battery using a battery charger. If your battery continues to fail even after charging, replace it.

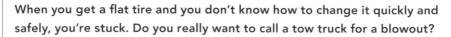

When you get a flat tire and you don't know how to change it quickly and safely, you're stuck. Do you really want to call a tow truck for a blowout?

[1] If you are driving, pull off the road to a safe place where there is good visibility for other drivers (*i.e.*, don't park on a corner—try to find a flat stretch of road). Make sure that the ground is level—never attempt to change a tire on an incline.

[2] Switch on your hazards and place a red warning-triangle behind your car to warn other motorists.

[3] Put the emergency brake on and put the car into first gear (or "P" on an automatic).

[4] Passengers should leave the car and stand on the grass shoulder well away from the car and from oncoming traffic.

[5] Remove the spare tire, tire iron, and jack from the trunk.

[6] If the wheel has a hubcap, remove it with a screwdriver or the beveled end of the tire iron.

[7] Use the lug-wrench end of the tire iron to loosen two pairs of nuts diagonally opposite each other (usually turning them counter-clockwise). You may have to use your foot for extra leverage if the nuts are particularly stiff.

[8] Place the jack under the car behind the wheel. Check your manual to see where it should go, otherwise you could damage the trim.

[9] Jack up the car until the wheel is about six inches off the ground (don't stop when the flat tire is off the ground, because the fully inflated spare will be thicker and will therefore require greater clearance).

[10] Remove the nuts and slide the wheel off horizontally. Put the nuts in your pocket or in the hubcap to stop them from rolling away (or worse, rolling underneath the car).

[11] Do not lie under the car or place any part of your body underneath it; if the car slips off the jack you could be seriously injured.

[12] Line up the holes in the center of the spare tire rim with the bolts, and slide on the tire as far as it will go. Hand-tighten the nuts.

[13] Lower the car and remove the jack, then tighten the nuts completely using the tire iron, working with diagonally opposite pairs, as before.

[14] Replace the hubcap and secure the flat tire and tools in the trunk.

[15] Visit a garage as soon as possible to get the flat tire repaired and to have your wheels rebalanced.

PARALLEL PARK

If you've been driving for years and you still can't parallel park, take a few minutes to read these instructions and you'll never have to worry about squeezing into a tight spot again.

[1] Use your indicators to signal the direction in which you intend to park. If you have to wait for another car to vacate the space, wait behind the space (not in front!). The space between cars should be about six feet longer than your car.

[2] When the space is empty, pull forward so that your rear tires are lined up with the rear bumper of the car in front. There should be about a two-foot gap between your two cars.

[3] Look back to check for traffic.

[4] When the road is clear, put the car into reverse and start moving backward very slowly. As soon as the car starts moving, turn the steering wheel completely in the direction of the curb (you need to move the car as slowly as you can while turning the wheel as fast as you can). Moving the wheels while the car is stationary is called "dry steering" and should be avoided, as it wears the tires and may damage the power steering.

[5] Back slowly into the space until the back of your car's front door is level with the rear bumper of the car in front; your car should by now be at a forty-five-degree angle with the curb. Now turn the wheel in the opposite direction as you continue to move slowly backward.

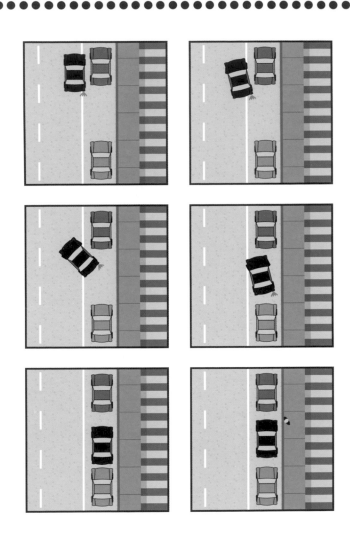

[6] Straighten the wheel and move backward or forward in the space to center yourself and to leave enough space for the cars in front and behind to maneuver.

[7] Before leaving your vehicle, check that it is no more than twelve inches from the curb, otherwise you risk receiving a ticket.

Exiting the space

Back up the car as far as you can go without hitting the car behind.

Check for traffic. When the road is clear, signal and begin moving forward slowly, while turning the steering wheel away from the curb completely as fast as you can. This should be enough to get the front of your car clear of the vehicle in front. If so, turn the wheel the other way as you pull out. If not, reverse slowly again while turning the wheel toward the curb until the front of your car is clear.

If you live in an area with heavy annual snowfall, by far the safest option is to take a specialized winter-driving-skills course. However, below are the basic guidelines for driving on snow and ice.

[1] Before setting off, make sure your car is in good condition and is equipped with snow tires.

[2] Clear pathways for your wheels on your driveway. Try inching forward and backward for a while, or else you may have to get digging (see page 127).

[3] Add sand or grit to the pathways.

[4] Do not accelerate quickly. On winter roads, take everything steadily.

[5] If you still have difficulty getting started, try easing forward in second gear.

[6] If the car is stuck, ease forward a little in second gear, then release the accelerator so that the car "rocks" back a little. Repeat the process, taking care to go easy on the accelerator, so that gradually you inch the car out.

[7] Keep your speed down considerably: you should be driving well below the speed limit.

[8] Keep twice as much distance from other cars as you would do in dry conditions.

[9] Anticipate the road: look ahead for obstacles, hazards, and corners in the road.

[10] As you approach a corner, reduce your speed. You should have your foot off the break before you begin to turn the steering wheel so that all four wheels can grip the road properly on the turn.

[11] Steer steadily around the corner and accelerate gently out of it.

[12] Build up momentum gradually on flat stretches before climbing a hill. Too much gas and you risk spinning your wheels.

What To Do If You Skid

[1] Steer into the direction the car is skidding, not against it.

[2] Fight the instinct to break hard, as this will reduce the grip of the wheels on the road.

[3] Ease off the brake and accelerate very gently into the skid.

[4] As you feel the wheels gaining their grip on the road, you can begin to adjust your steering accordingly.

What To Do As You Approach A Red Light

[1] Reduce your speed early on as you approach lights.

[2] Bring the car to as slow a speed as you can gradually.

[3] Avoid stopping completely if possible.

Packing a suitcase correctly is a juggling act between desire and necessity, of maximizing space and minimizing creases.

[1] Place heavy, bulky items on the bottom, followed by the non-creasable items, then delicates such as blouses and shirts.

[2] Mix and match so that most of your clothes can be worn in combination.

[3] If you travel with more than one pair of shoes, wear the heaviest to cut down on weight (but make sure they are comfortable for flying). Pack shoes in a plastic bag to avoid odors and dirtying your clothes.

[4] Pack lots of lightweight layers and you will be prepared for hot and cold temperatures. Strip off a layer if it's warm and add a few if you're chilly.

[5] Spread everything that you intend to pack on your bed or a table first.

[6] Fit underwear and socks down the sides of the case when it is full, rather than filling up valuable space in the middle.

[7] Use travel-size toiletries to save space and place them in a plastic bag to protect your clothes from leaks.

[8] Don't pack valuables (money, keys, passports, travel documents, medication, etc.) in any luggage that will leave your possession during your journey.

[9] Rolling clothes is a good way to reduce wrinkles. This has always been the standard way of filling a backpack.

[10] Consider what you will be bringing back from your trip and leave enough space (and weight allowance, if you are flying). Also, consider buying some cheap clothes while abroad and discarding them over there.

[11] If in doubt, leave it out. You are more likely to take too much than too little. If you run out of clothes, the inconvenience of a little hand washing far outweighs the hassle of dragging around ten pounds of redundant gear.

[12] Pack fragile items in the center of the case, surrounded and protected by soft clothes.

[13] Test the weight of the case once it is packed. If flying, remember that you may have to travel a long way from the check-in desk to the terminal (especially on a budget airline), so you must be able to carry or wheel your case long distances. Picking it up for five seconds in your bedroom is not the same experience! If you are unable to carry your case, remove non-essentials or split the contents into two cases.

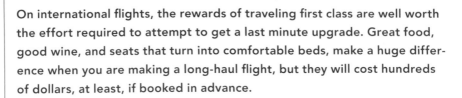

GET AN AIRLINE UPGRADE

On international flights, the rewards of traveling first class are well worth the effort required to attempt to get a last minute upgrade. Great food, good wine, and seats that turn into comfortable beds, make a huge difference when you are making a long-haul flight, but they will cost hundreds of dollars, at least, if booked in advance.

Securing An Upgrade When You Book

This can be tricky, but if you (or your travel agent) add an OSI (other significant information) message onto your booking record it can make a difference to how you travel. For example, if you are a representative of a commercially important organization, this should be added to your record.

Frequent Fliers

This is one of the most common ways of securing an upgrade. If an airline can see that you have built up a loyalty, they are more likely to want to reward you.

Look And Act The Part

Next time you are in an airport lounge, take a look at the first class customers. Make a note of how they are dressed, their luggage, and their manner. If you are traveling in sweats and sneakers, along with your three young children, you are almost certainly not going to be offered an upgrade to first class. Dress well; be polite, friendly, and amenable. Airport personnel are used to difficult encounters with stressed travelers. Be an exception and you may just make enough of an impression on the clerk to get yourself a reward.

Pick Your Moment

Approach the first-class desk early enough and you will at least stand a chance of getting your name down on the list for upgrades. Otherwise, try talking

politely to the gate clerk at a quiet moment. Clerks have the authority to up-grade passengers, but are unlikely to do so if you ask in front of an audience.

Getting Upgraded While On Board

Always be prepared to move seats if asked to do so by airline personnel: it may be that they are offering you a seat in first class. Likewise, if you have a valid reason why you wish to be moved away from the passenger next to you, ask discreetly enough and you may get lucky. It's worth remembering that the airline will only have so many first class meals on board: if you are asking for an upgrade at this stage, explain that you are prepared to forego the meal if necessary.

AVOID JET LAG

It is impossible to completely eradicate the disruption caused to your internal organs and body clock from traveling halfway around the world. Fortunately, there are plenty of precautions you can take to minimize the impact.

Be Prepared

Pre-flight preparation is one of the most important ways of combating jet lag. The more organized and relaxed you are before your trip, the better. Get plenty of sleep, avoid drinking alcohol, and get adequate exercise during the week prior to traveling. Anything that puts negative stress on your mind and body will be magnified after your journey.

Direction

There is some evidence that the direction in which you travel (east or west) makes a difference, and that flying westward causes less disruption than flying eastward.

Day Or Night

Many travelers feel that a long-haul flight during daytime is easier, since they would be awake anyway. Nighttime travel is likely to cause disrupted sleep, although potentially considerably less boredom and restlessness.

Stay Hydrated

Drink lots of fluids, as the pressurized cabin atmosphere is dry. Water is best. Avoid coffee and tea. Alcohol is a big no-no. Not only will alcohol dehydrate you, the intoxicating effects are magnified.

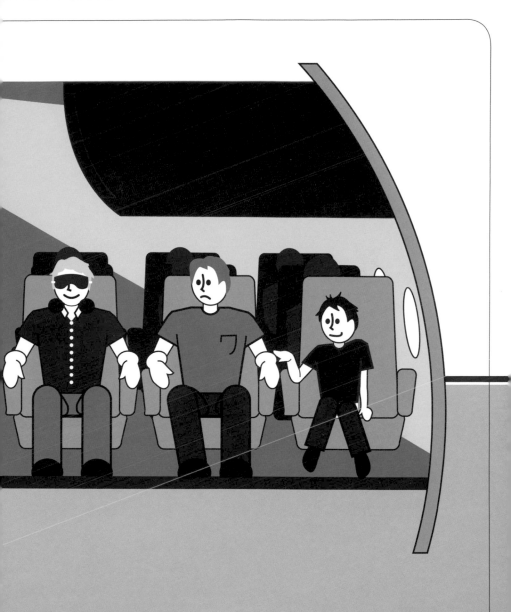

Sleep-aids

Stock up on eyeshades, inflatable neck rests, pillows, and earplugs to help you get some quality shuteye. Remove your shoes before sleeping, as your feet will swell. Avoid sleeping pills, because when knocked out cold your body may be dangerously inactive for a long time. It is safer to sleep less soundly so that your body can move a little. Sleeping pills often cause dehydration.

Stay Active

Exercise regularly during the flight—get up and walk around and do stretches, all of which helps to keep you energized, improves circulation, and reduces the risk of blood clots.

Anti-Jet Lag Diet

Some people report the benefits of following a special anti-jet lag diet in the days prior to traveling, which often consists of alternating between feasting and fasting, and between high-protein and high-carbohydrate meals, to gradu-ally get your body used to different eating times. One of the major causes of disorientation is that after your flight, your digestive system will have to adjust to eating during what it still thinks is the middle of the night.

Take off for a hike with a compass and teach yourself how to read a map. It's a great way to burn calories while learning a new skill.

Scale

Most maps work to a consistent scale so that every distance and dimension is shrunk by the same amount. The scale is written in the key that explains the other symbols, something like this: 1:25,000. This means that one unit on the map corresponds to 25,000 units on the ground. So if you measure a distance between two places on the map with a ruler and get 4 inches, in reality that distance is 4 x 25,000 inches = 100,000 inches, which is about 1.58 miles.

Grid References

Maps are covered with grid lines that criss-cross to split the map into squares. Each grid line is numbered. Grid references are used to locate squares and places. A four-figure grid reference is used to locate a square. For example, to find the square represented by the grid reference 2345, you would go horizontally along the map to grid line 23, then follow the line vertically up the page until you reached grid line 45. Where the grid lines cross is the bottom left-hand corner of the square.

Six-figure grid references are used to pinpoint places. For example, 236 458 would be inside the square 2345. Once you have located the square, you split it into a hundred squares (ten by ten), then move along horizontally six mini-grid lines, and vertically up eight mini-grid lines to pinpoint your target.

Measuring Curves

Often, you need to know the distance between two points while following a road or track (rather than going straight, "as the crow flies"). If the road meanders, you can lay a piece of string along it, then measure the string to get the actual journey distance.

Hills And Mountains

The shape of the land (topography) is shown by joining places of equal height above sea level with thin brown contour lines. The closer the contours, the greater the incline. Contours are often drawn for every ten feet of elevation (otherwise the whole map would be brown), but they aren't all labeled. To work out the increment, you must count the number of contours between two labeled contours, and divide the elevation difference between the two contours by the total number.

Using A Compass

In most maps, North is at the top of the page, and South at the bottom. To work out which direction to travel, draw a line between your starting point and destination. Place the middle of the compass on your starting point with North pointing vertically up the page, then read the direction at the point where the line crosses the compass edge. Be aware of contour lines between the two points—you may have to climb a mountain (or go round it) to reach your destination.

Whether you want to take portraits or landscapes, the basic elements of lighting, framing, and focusing are vital ingredients of photographic composition.

[1] Understand your camera and learn how to use it—read the manual. Keep things simple, but don't let your camera do everything for you. The more you become involved in the mechanics of taking the photograph, the greater control you will have over the final results.

[2] Choose your location and visit it at different times of the day to appreciate how the lighting changes. Shoot at times of greatest contrast—early morning and late afternoon are good times for this. This also avoids harsh shadows, giving you a more diffused light source. Think about the direction of the light, its quality, the contrasts it provides, and the shadows it creates.

[3] Be flexible and always on the lookout for good subjects, rather than hidebound to what you intended to shoot.

[4] Look for the best position and experiment with different levels of perspective. Often, a high vantage point is preferable.

[5] Include a feature in the foreground to add a sense of depth and scale to your photograph.

[6] Use a tripod and a cable shutter release to allow you to use slower shutter speeds and smaller apertures for greater contrast and increased sharpness.

[7] Focus creatively. Rather than always setting a focus at infinity so that everything is in focus, experiment with the depth-of-field marks on your camera lens so that your photo has depth. Make sure that the horizon is horizontal.

[8] Don't center the subject for every shot. The rule of thirds is a simple way to keep your compositions interesting. Divide the field of view with two vertical lines and two horizontal ones (like a tic-tac-toe board) and position your subject where two lines meet (now you have four other points to choose from instead of the center). Try placing the horizon along one of the third lines rather than in the middle.

[9] Notice "leading lines." These are elements of the composition that make the eye move. For example, a railroad track will draw the eye along it—leading lines may be something you wish to use or avoid, but you must be aware of them before you can make your choice.

[10] The most common mistake when photographing people is to stand too far away. Getting in closer can improve a portrait or group photograph tenfold.

If you ever find yourself seriously lost, this could come in very useful. Otherwise, it's an interesting and fun exercise.

Finding Your Direction By Day

This is relatively simple if you construct a simple variation on a sundial, as outlined below.

What You Will Need

A straight pole about a yard in length

A length of string

Two sharp objects—sticks or rocks, for example

Method

[1] Beginning in the morning, well before midday, select a clear, flat piece of ground.

[2] Fix the long pole firmly into the ground.

[3] Fix one of the sharp objects into the ground at the point at which the shadow ends.

[4] Tie the other sharp object to the length of string and fix the other end to the pole. The string needs to be exactly long enough to reach the central pole and the end of the morning shadow, marked by the smaller object.

[5] Use the tied sharp object on the string to draw a semi-circle into the ground.

[6] Mark the shadow at regular intervals. At noon, when the sun is highest in the sky, the shadow will point to the north.

[7] When the shadow is once more the same length as your semi-circle, mark the spot again.

[8] The morning spot you marked points west and the last point you marked will point east. North (in case you didn't estimate the time correctly) will be the midway point between the two on your semi-circle.

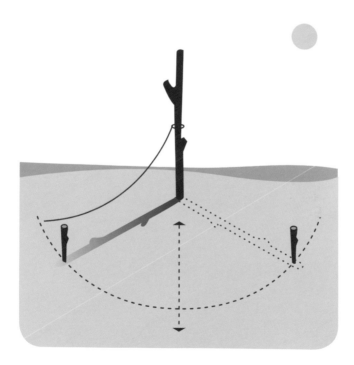

Finding Your Direction At Night

Lost at night? Let the stars be your guide. As with finding your direction by day, this method relies on a good clear sky.

If there's one constellation that most people are likely to know, it's the Big Dipper.

Draw an imaginary line with your finger that extends from the top two stars of the Big Dipper. You will come to a bright star called Polaris, or the North Star, that is never more than one degree beyond true North. This is located at the very tip of the handle of a second constellation known as the Little Dipper.

Practice spotting the Big Dipper and the Little Dipper in the night sky. Once you can find them easily, it should be a simple process to find the North Star and work out which way is North.

CHOP DOWN A TREE

Felling a tree is dangerous. If you are going to attempt this task yourself, ensure you have taken the following precautions.

[1] Check that the tree is completely free from electrical power lines. If it is not, you will need to bring in experts for the job.

[2] Decide which way the tree is likely to fall. This is determined by the angle at which the tree is growing, which side of the tree carries the weightiest branches, and the direction of the wind, as much as where you do your cutting.

[3] Ensure the entire area has been cleared of people, pets, and vehicles. Even neighboring trees can make the process more hazardous.

[4] Before you begin to cut, decide how you will move clear of the falling trunk.

[5] Don't run with the power saw in your hands, even if it is switched off. Put it down and then move away from the falling tree.

[6] Wear safety goggles and heavy-duty gloves.

[7] Always cut away from your body and limbs when using a chainsaw. Don't saw between your legs.

Felling A Tree From The Base

Fell a small tree with one cut through the trunk with the chainsaw, or else slice through smaller sections of the trunk one at a time, so that you are left with more manageable logs for storing as firewood.

For trunks thicker than about six inches, you will need to make several cuts.

[1] Cut out a chunk from the side of the trunk the tree will fall into. Make the lower cut first, then the top cut, both of which should meet at about a third of the way into the trunk at a forty-five-degree angle.

[2] Now focus on the opposite side of the trunk. Aim the chainsaw a little higher than the lower cut of the chunk, and do not cut all the way through to meet it. You will need to leave a thin section that will ease the tree's fall safely.

[3] If the tree does not fall, you can drive plastic wedges into the trunk with a sledgehammer to help the process along. Do so gently and cautiously, as driving the wedges too hard into the trunk risks bringing the tree down on you.

A modern two-person tent is easy to assemble. It usually consists of a combined tent and flysheet, three multi-section fiberglass poles (two long and one shorter), steel pegs, and guy ropes. Make sure you practice at home before you go camping for the first time.

[1] Find a level place free from rocks and other sharp objects, which may damage the floor of the tent. Avoid pitching near trees.

[2] Spread the tent out flat on the ground with the zippers closed.

[3] Assemble the sections of the three fiberglass poles. The sections are joined together by an elastic cord running through the center, so all you have to do is fit the ends into each other.

[4] Thread the poles through the pole sleeves on the outside of the tent; if the poles become detached, carefully fit them back together inside the sleeve and resume threading. The two longer poles thread diagonally across the tent, crossing in the middle to create the dome; the shorter pole threads across one side, to form the entrance.

[5] At all four edges of the tent there are plastic eyelets, each with three holes. Bend each long pole in a semi-circular shape and fit the ends into the inner of the three eyelet holes. Bend the shorter pole into a semi-circular shape and fit each end into a middle eyelet hole. The tension of the poles, held in place by the eyelets, will keep the tent rigid.

[6] With the door zip closed, peg down the four corners of the floor with a peg in each outer eyelet hole.

[7] Drive pegs into the ground a few feet away from the tent, and attach the guy ropes (the tent will have 6 to 8 of them). Ensure the guy ropes and the pegs form a ninety-degree angle, so that the guy ropes won't pull the pegs out of the ground. Tighten all the guy ropes.

[8] Attach the dome cover to the top of the tent (this goes over a mesh ventilation area).

BUILD A SHELTER (IN THE WILD)

If you ever find yourself lost in the wild, and too far from help to hike in a day or two, building a good shelter to protect you from the worst of the elements and enable you to rest may mean the difference between life and death.

Choose Your Location

Whatever the weather conditions, you will need to find the right place to construct your shelter. Avoid exposed areas and look for a shaded spot beneath trees, preferably on higher ground.

Before You Start

Before you decide what kind of shelter to build, bear in mind the following basic tips.

[1] Don't overdo it. The smaller the better when it comes to a temporary shelter. The bigger it is, the harder it will be to build and to heat.

[2] If the temperature is dropping, you will need to build in ventilation so that you can keep a fire going inside your shelter. There is a risk from carbon monoxide if the smoke cannot escape.

[3] If the ground is covered with snow, only attempt a snow shelter if the snow is dense enough that it doesn't leave a deep footprint as you walk.

Building A Snow Shelter

Once you have ascertained that the snow is dense enough, the quickest way to shelter in the snow is to dig out rectangular blocks of snow until you have built a burrow-like tunnel, leaving enough snow overhead for a sturdy roof. Make several ventilation holes and dig the tunnel away from the wind so that the entrance stays free from drifting snow. Keep your tools with you just in case.

Building A Lean-to

Look for a large object such as a fallen tree trunk, a stump, or a large rock. Lay one large branch on the ground, raised by the object at one end. Now use this branch as a means of laying further smaller branches out, filling in holes and gaps with small twigs, leaves, moss, etc.

Building A Tepee

You need to find three fairly sizeable branches and fasten them together at the top with rope or whatever you can find. Spread the three legs out and use this framework to support as many more branches as you can find. Use anything small to fill in the gaps: twigs, leaves, moss, etc.

BUILD A CAMPFIRE

Knowing how to build a campfire in the wild makes the difference between dancing flames, warm meals, and camaraderie, and lying shivering and hungry in a sleeping bag.

Pitch Camp

Choose a suitable place to build your fire. It should be sandy or rocky, and preferably close to a source of sand or water, so that you can put out the fire quickly if necessary. It should also be dry, partially sheltered (too much wind will make the fire hard to light), and close to a source of tinder (dry material which ignites with a spark—wood shavings, feathers, paper, straw, etc.), kindling (twigs, small pieces of wood, etc.), and fuel (material which burns more slowly—thicker branches and logs, coal, twisted dry reeds, etc.).

Here are four common methods of fire building, each suitable for different conditions.

Tepee

Build tinder and fuel into a cone or tepee shape around a core of tinder or kindling. Light the middle. Air is drawn into the bottom of the tepee and, as the inside material burns, the outside branches fall into the center, so the fire requires little maintenance. Also, if the outside branches are damp, they will have a chance to dry before they burn.

Cross-ditch

If you are having difficulty lighting the fire, use a stick or knife to scrape a cross in the ground about a foot across and three-inches deep. Place lots of tinder in the center of the cross and build a tepee of kindling above. Light the tinder; as it burns, air is drawn through the cross and underneath the fire to provide oxygen for the flames.

Lean-to

Place a stick in the ground at a thirty-degree angle, pointing in the direction of the wind. Lean kindling on either side of this stick and place tinder deep inside. Light the tinder. As the fire progresses from the short to long sticks, add more kindling and fuel.

Terrace

Place two larger logs parallel and then lay several thinner logs across them to form a platform, leaving ventilation gaps in between the logs. Add a second layer at right angles to the last, using even thinner logs, and repeat until you have a terraced pyramid. Place tinder and kindling on top and light it. This fire burns from the top downward, so it requires less maintenance.

Before you break camp, ensure your fire is completely extinguished and cold to touch. Flick it with water and cover with non-flammable material like sand or dirt.

BAIT A FISHING HOOK

The thrill of your first catch is made all the sweeter if you have baited your own hook skillfully, and fooled a fish into taking the bait. There's more to it than skewering a worm on your hook. For starters, you want live bait to stay just that—alive, or at least to look alive.

Handle the worm as little as possible. Your hands are covered with telltale scents and amino acids that coat the worm and warn the fish away. Syringe-like devices are available which bait hooks automatically, without the angler having to touch the worm with his or her hands. Alternatively, you can wear disposable latex gloves.

Here are three ways of baiting worms. In the first diagram, the hook passes through the tip of the body, so that the tip reaches the tip of the hook.

In the second diagram, the worm has been threaded onto the hook lengthwise through its whole body—slimy yet effective, because not only does it follow the contour of the hook (hiding it), it is also very secure and will not fall off.

In the third diagram, the worm is attached in a concertina shape, and the hook passes through its body several times. This is secure and helps to give the illusion that the worm is alive, making it more inviting to the fish.

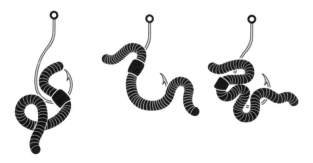

Bait crickets and grasshoppers in their backs behind the head.

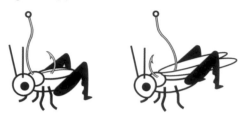

Bait minnows through the top of the mouth or underneath the dorsal fin.

When baiting with live fish, only handle them with wet hands, otherwise you will remove scales and slime and damage them. Do not hook live bait through the eyes. Not only is this an insecure method, but you want the baitfish to see the approaching fish because then it will dart about in an attempt to escape. This will excite the other fish, making it more aggressive, increasing your chances of a bite, and the frequency of bites.

In fly-fishing, artificial flies such as fur and feather are used as bait. Skillful casting gives the illusion that the bait is alive. Unlike spin-casting which uses a weight to pull the line out of the reel, fly-casting uses a heavier line and a back-and-forth rod action; it is these that provide the momentum.

Practice casting in an open space away from the water until you have mastered the technique. (A field of grass is ideal. Don't cast on asphalt, as this will damage your line.) Tie a little bright fly on the end of the line so you can see it.

[1] Pull twenty-five to thirty feet of line from the reel and lay it on the ground in front of you.

[2] Hold the rod handle firmly in your palm, close your fingers around it, and place your thumb on top. Keep the rod butt under your wrist and along your forearm.

[3] Stand facing your target, with your weight on the balls of your feet. If your target is at twelve o'clock (relative to the elevated rod), when you cast you will move the rod briskly between eleven and one o'clock.

[4] Hold the line in your left hand and keep it tight during the cast, just above waist level.

[5] Begin with a swift stroke that sweeps the rod to eleven o'clock and then to one o'clock, and stop abruptly. This will make the line flick behind you.

[6] Watch the line. As it straightens behind you and becomes horizontal (but before it touches the ground), flick again to eleven o'clock and stop abruptly there. This will make the line flick forward and land at twelve o'clock in front of you.

[7] The longer your line, the longer it will take for the line to straighten out behind you, so the longer you should leave between forward and backward casts. If your line makes a cracking noise, it is a sign that you should wait longer between casts.

[8] For a short cast aim about four feet above the ground; for longer casts, aim higher. Practice distance by setting up targets on the ground; modify your cast and aim accordingly.

[9] During the cast the tip of your rod should travel in a straight line. If you use too much force the tip will drop down, the line will form a "tailing loop," and the fly will land off target.

[10] When you are confident on grass, and you instinctively know what a good cast feels like through your rod, you are ready to cast on water.

INDEX